ED. Bill Watterson

GOD'S
LEADERS
FOR
TOMORROW'S
WORLD

Third Edition

Harold R. Eberle
Worldcast Publishing, Yakima, Washington

God's Leaders for Tomorrow's World
Third Edition

© 2003 by Harold R. Eberle

Worldcast Publishing Company
P.O. Box 10653, Yakima, WA 98909-1653, USA
(509) 248-5837
www.worldcastpublishing.com
office@worldcastpublishing.com

First Edition: First Printing, 1993
                      Second Printing, 1995
Second Edition: First Printing, 1998
Third Edition: First Printing, 2003

ISBN 1-882523-21-0

Cataloging in Publication Data
Eberle, Harold R. 1954-
   God's Leaders for Tomorrow's World, Third Edition
   1. Christian leadership. 2. Leadership. I. Title.
   BV652.1   291.61

Cover by Paul Jones

All biblical quotations are taken from the New American Standard Bible © 1978, The Lockman Foundation, La Habra, California 90631.

Printed in the United States of America

All inquiries about reprinting and/or translating into other languages should be addressed to Worldcast Publishing.

Credits and Thanks

I would like to thank every leader who has spoken into my own life, discipled me at various times, and invested themselves in my work, including John King, Dan Reber, Chris Blackmore, and Ray Fredericks. My thanks also go to Pastor Jim Leuschen who deserves credit for the basic concepts on authority presented in Chapter Two. It was Pastor David Shirk who planted the seeds of understanding for the principles on *metron*.

James Bryson greatly improved my communication skills through his tedious editing. Annette Bradley is my final editor with a sharp eye for detail. Thanks to each of you.

Table of Contents

Introduction

At a critical moment in my life, a strong Christian leader asked me, "Do you want others to follow you?" Of course, my answer was in the affirmative. Then he said, "Become worth following."

There is a *process* involved in becoming an effective leader, requiring training, experience, and maturing. Nothing can replace the ongoing work of pruning and nourishing which only God can accomplish over the course of many years.

Yet, occasionally our progress receives a boost by the help and input of others. Jesus said the pupil will become as his teacher (Luke 6:40). For this reason, I spent several years of my life studying the lives of great men and women of God in history. I also carefully watched those alive today who are influential in the Body of Christ and who are accomplishing mighty works for our Lord. It soon became evident that certain ways of thinking and attitudes were common to all successful leaders. The wise pupil will emulate those qualities.

Leadership, however, is not merely taught, but caught. For this reason, Moses laid his hands on Joshua actually to impart his authority (Num. 27:18-20). Paul wrote of his desire to impart grace to those who followed him (Rom. 1:11). It is through such a transmission of divine anointing that leaders arise.

I write so that you may obtain a quality of leadership, a spirit of holiness, a clearer standard, and a greater measure of grace. To be a leader, you must think as a leader. To be a man or woman of God, you must be God's man or woman. I pray that grace will be transmitted through these pages into your spirit. Catch what you need to catch and determine to become who God created you to be.

You may notice in the following pages that I predominantly use the male gender pronouns in order to simplify communication. However, please understand that I believe in and recognize men and women in leadership roles.

Chapter One
Purpose at the Front

People want leaders.

People want someone in whom to believe. They both desire and need a person to respect—a champion of the faith—someone who stands for what they themselves believe. If they have an individual to whom they can point as an example of success, a person who has gone through the trials of life, yet has overcome using the very principles to which they hold, then they can continue believing and hoping that they, too, will succeed. A perfect example is when David defeated Goliath, inspiring his Jewish brethren to rise and conquer their enemies (I Sam. 17:41-54). In this manner a leader catalyzes faith in the hearts of the people he leads. Without a leader, it is difficult for most people to believe in themselves.

A leader also provides and releases love. People can sense whether or not a certain leader cares about them. It is one thing to have a peer or a spouse or a child love you. It fulfills an entirely different need, however, to have a person you respect give his life for your well-being. It creates self-worth. It dissolves guilt. It stimulates love among all involved.

In addition, leaders provide a standard by which men and women measure themselves. When a trust-worthy leader speaks, listeners judge their own beliefs according to what the person whom they respect is saying. If they agree, their own beliefs are strengthened. If they disagree, they either reevaluate and change their views, or they reevaluate and become stronger in their opposing views. Either way, a leader is an instrument by which men and women clarify their own thoughts. To listen to, read the books by, or spend time with a leader is to commit to a process whereby one's mind and emotions become established. A leader, then, is a catalyst toward personal stability and security in one's own beliefs.

Even more important, a leader provides purpose and energy for life. Without a vision and direction, people wander. They go through life discouraged and disillusioned. The plain truth is that the vast majority of people were created to be followers—and every one of us are followers in most areas of our lives. No individual has enough energy to discipline himself and work every day while staying at the forefront in every area of life. A leader pushes through difficulties in some specific area to make a way for others to follow. In doing so, they provide direction and energy for others. Only by following such leaders can people be productive, happy, and blessed.

Further, leaders unite people. We were created with a need to belong and work together. Without leadership, this is impossible. Anything significant that has been accomplished in society has been done through the cooperative effort of many. Leaders are needed to focus the labors of people and simply to help them live together in peace and harmony.

Finally, people want a leader to tell them what to do. This may sound domineering, but I do not mean it in that way. Every person—including leaders themselves—needs direction. They need others to encourage them, point the way, and reaffirm their own decisions. The apostle Paul wrote:

How will they go unless they are sent?

(Rom. 10:15a)

Paul made this statement to Christians who should know God's will for their individual lives. Concerning them, he stated that even they will not step out in faith unless someone encourages them to do so. It is true: A leader's job is to tell people what to do. I am not advocating control nor manipulation. A leader simply is the one who has the authority and ability to send others. Therefore, he helps them fulfill what God has placed them on this earth to do.

I have found in my own life that being aware of "these purposes for leadership" is essential. When I first accepted the leadership position over a church, I did not have much visible fruit to show for my labors, and it was difficult to support my family financially. Well-meaning friends, whether or not they stated it verbally, would sometimes look at me with a question in their minds: "When are you going to get a *real* job?" That was a question I had to answer for myself again and again, for my own well-being. Of course, I am not for people loafing around or using ministry as an excuse for inactivity. But I found that I had to define my purpose as a leader before I could focus my energies and actually accomplish what God was calling me to do.

Just as a businessperson offers a product or service to the public, so also every leader has something to offer the people. The grocery store owner makes food available to the local residents. A secretary provides her skills and time. A doctor provides his or her education, training, and wisdom. With no less clarity of purpose, a leader has something to give. You cannot load it into a truck and ship it to the store across town. It cannot be quantified nor marked with a price tag. A leader gives that which cannot be seen. Yet, what leadership produces is the visible fruit of changed lives, fulfillment, healthy relationships among people, faith in people's hearts, and the very structure of the society in which we live. The leadership business is the most important business in the world.

Chapter Two
Four Lines of Authority

Authority structure pervades everything in this world. If it were not for authority, you would not know on which side of the road to drive your car, or whether or not you should stop at the red light. Your car never would have been made at a factory, because people cannot be organized to work together without a leadership structure. The home in which you live is established and protected by authority. Not only is your home protected from enemies of another country, but neither can your neighbor simply walk in without your permission. The grocery store in which you shop is dependent upon authority to carry on its daily activities; otherwise, employees would not know what to do and customers simply could walk out the door with merchandise. Everything you do throughout the day is permeated by authority structures.

The Bible shows us four distinct lines of authority in the world: the government, the Church, the family, and the individual. Each of these entities is responsible before God. Let's examine each of these.

In Romans, Chapter 13, we find clear instructions about how we should recognize the authority of the established government. The Apostle Paul wrote:

Let every person be in subjection to the

> *governing authorities. For there is no au-*
> *thority except from God, and those which*
> *exist are established by God.* (Rom. 13:1)

The context of this verse is leaders who govern society. This government does not include merely political
leaders, but all authority that is delegated to establish
civil order. This extends all the way from the king or
president down to the local community, business, or
school. God is behind such leadership. Of course, not
all natural governmental systems are upholding godly
principles, but we—as Bible-believers—must ac-
knowledge that God Himself is the One who estab-
lishes governmental order.

The second line of authority is the Church. God
gives clear instructions in the New Testament about
the function and roles of elders and all leaders within
the Church. Several Bible verses speak about authority and submission within the Body of Christ (i.e., I
Peter 5:5). Christians are exhorted:

> *Obey your leaders, and submit to them;*
> *for they keep watch over your souls, as*
> *those who will give an account.*
> (Heb. 13:17)

Submission is a meaningless word apart from authority. This authority is from God and we are told that
the leaders will be held accountable to God.

Third is the authority which God has ordained for
the family unit. The father is the head of his family (I
Cor. 11:3), a husband and wife are called to rule
together, and the children are to obey their parents

(Eph. 6:1-2). So important is it for children to honor their parents that it was recorded as one of the Ten Commandments (Ex. 20:12). Paul exhorted children to honor their parents, stating God's promised reward, "that it may be well with you and you may live long upon the earth" (Eph. 6:2-3). God established the family unit from the beginning, and there is a divine authority that works through it.

The fourth line of authority is to the individual. Every human being has a free will and each is independently responsible before God for his or her own actions. People have authority and responsibility for their own lives.

It is important that we recognize all four of these lines of authority and understand that each comes from God. We must respect these. People cause chaos and get into trouble when they cross the God-ordained authority lines. For example, the government is violating God-ordained authority when it tries to control the Church. Conversely, we have seen throughout history that the Church has gotten into trouble when she has tried to control the established government.

I am not teaching isolationism nor noninvolvement. On the contrary, we must make an *influence* across authority lines. The Church is to shine the light, be the salt of the earth, and do all in her power to influence the government to follow godly paths. Similarly, each individual should attempt to influence their family in a positive fashion.

It is the "usurping of authority" against which I am teaching. Every established authority is established by God and, therefore, must be left accountable to God. That authority must not be violated.

This means that the Church has a certain line of authority, but she must not violate the authority God has established within the family or for the individual. She should teach, and Church leaders even may rebuke harshly at times, but she must not dictate what the families or individuals have to do in violation of their free wills.

Similarly, the family must allow each individual member to make decisions for his or her own personal life. Each individual must respect the established structure of the family. No one person should be allowed to control the Church or violate the government's authority. Each line of authority must be respected and recognized as accountable to God.

When people cross their line of authority, then they are no longer backed by God's authority nor His power. For example, if the family dictates to a member what he or she is to do, in violation of the individual's free will, then they are controlling and dominating in an evil manner. Similarly, if a church leader starts demanding that families or individuals do things which should be decided only by themselves, then authority is being abused and God is not behind it. Evil forces (which we will explain as we continue) begin where God's authority ends.

Now the question of disobedience to authority arises. For example, should a Christian go against the dictates of the established government? When should an individual go against his spiritual leaders? I hesitate to answer the question, lest people take my understanding as an absolute rule to be applied mechanically. As each person is responsible before God, each must decide for his own life. Similarly, the

Church is responsible before God, therefore, she must determine God's will in each situation that is faced. Please understand this...we are talking about principles here, not legalistic dictates.

There are times when civil disobedience is appropriate, for we see in the Book of Acts that the early disciples preached the Gospel even though the governmental authorities forbade them to do so (Acts 4:15-20). Note that the disciples were not exerting their authority over the local authorities. Rather, they were claiming the authority which God already had given to them. This was not a case of the disciples crossing into the government's authority, but rather, the governmental officials crossing into the Church's authority and telling her not to speak what God had commissioned her to declare. The disciples were not violating authority, but they were claiming the authority which was rightfully theirs.

This principle of claiming one's God-given authority holds true in the individual's life, as well. Every individual must have responsibility for his own life. If the family or the Church begins to dictate what the individual should do, in violation of individual freedom, then that person has a right to disobey. He is not being disobedient to God in exercising that right, because the family or Church, in such cases, has no authority from God to be domineering or controlling.

In all such circumstances, it is God-given authority that we must recognize. There is not just one line of authority, but four.

This is important because some leaders have been guilty of abusing authority and dominating people. Others have gone to the opposite extreme and made themselves timid because they were afraid of becoming overbearing. Both of these problems can be overcome simply by recognizing and respecting the four lines of authority God has established.

Those who are abusive need to realize that their authority ends where another's begins. Most cases of evil control and manipulation do not occur because a leader was too forceful or strong. Rather, they are the results of someone exercising authority outside of that which God has given.

At the other extreme are those who hold back from speaking and saying things because they are afraid of controlling others wrongfully. They, too, will find freedom only by hearing the truth. Freedom from evil control and manipulation does not come by making oneself wishy-washy. On the contrary, a person can be very bold and even forceful without releasing evil forces. There are many things over which leaders should take control. The key is that they stay within the authority God has given them. When a person knows he is in a God-given role, then he is not weak, but rather confident.

Leaders must know this. Only if they decide when and where God has given them authority will they fulfill God's purposes for their lives. Only as they respect the other lines of authority will they be confident within their own. As they bring their daily decisions into alignment with all four authority lines, God's authority works in their lives and, as a consequence, peace and order reign.

Chapter Three
Believe in Leadership

There is a philosophy common in parts of the church-world today that is contrary to the emergence and survival of leaders. It sees all Christians as equals with no person rising above another. People are taught to relate to one another only on a co-equal basis, with no one person exercising authority over anyone else.

Two opposing views are formed in the mind of the average person: (1) people should relate to each other *only* on an equal basis; or (2) some *should* rise above and exercise authority over others.

These two philosophies of life can be applied to any and all areas, such as the family unit, government, business, sports, finances, and, of course, church structure. In the home, parents would find it impossible to pay the bills or even cook dinner if someone did not have the authority to make the necessary decisions. When we talk about a specific business or a sports team, we immediately envision a boss on the job and a coach or captain on the team. We cannot conceive of being successful in most endeavors of life without establishing some authority structure.

When our two philosophies of life are applied to economics, we develop two entirely different systems, one called *communism* and the other *capitalism*. Communism sees all people as equals and attempts to reflect this with economic progress being shared equally by all. Capitalism gives individuals the freedom to accept personal responsibility and progress financially according to their own productivity, wisdom, and talents.

We have seen in history the pitfalls of both economic systems. Indeed, we do want to see the needs of every human being met, as communism theoretically attempts to do. Unfortunately, through that system, both personal responsibility and incentive are diminished and, hence, all suffer. On the other side, capitalism also has its problems, as it gives opportunity for people to dominate and oppress those less fortunate.

When we look in the Bible, we discover God's economic system. In both the Old and New Testaments, He puts forth principles whereby people should be rewarded according to their labors. The Jews developed a clear capitalistic philosophy. In the New Testament, we read that a man who does not work should not be allowed to eat (II Thess. 3:10-12), and that the Christian faith demands that people must take personal responsibility to provide for their own families (I Tim. 5:8). Please research for yourself the Scriptures on this subject. It is important! The structure of capitalism was developed from the Bible.

Some people may object, saying, "But I also can see communistic principles in the Bible." It is true that the early disciples experienced such love that they were stirred to sell their possessions, even their houses, and give to one another. However, we are identifying in our discussion here the means to such ends. Yes, God wants all to be blessed, but it is to be accomplished through right attitudes in people's hearts. The society in which the first disciples lived was capitalistic, but the Spirit of God stirred in their hearts to give freely to those in need.

Karl Marx, by advancing the fundamentals of communism, attempted to *force* equality into being. I draw from Marx's own writings when I say that he vowed to overthrow anything pertaining to the Christian philosophy of life. Make no mistake about this: the communistic philosophy, wherein people are *forced* into relationships of equality, is wrong!

God is a capitalist...however, He opposes domination and oppression. His Word teaches us that those who are blessed financially should give to those in need (I Tim. 6:17-18). The Holy Spirit works upon the hearts of people, stirring them to help those less fortunate—sometimes even at great personal sacrifice. The philosophy which stems from God's nature is that which allows people to take personal responsibility and advance accordingly, but the Spirit pervading this philosophy is that of giving and helping others.

Now, let's turn our attention back to the structure within the Body of Christ. Some Christians today have accepted (without realizing it) the "communistic philosophy" when it comes to relationships within the Church. They rightfully see the need for all Christians to be treated equally and respected as priests unto God. However, they do not realize that such relationships are not established by an outward structure, but through appropriate heart attitudes. As a consequence of this misunderstanding, they tend to coerce people into equality relationships, and—consciously

15

or unconsciously—they undermine leaders and God-given motivation.

God is for leadership.

In Old Testament times, whenever the Jewish people were in trouble, God would put His Spirit upon a certain man or woman and anoint him/her with His authority to lead the people to victory. Moses and Joshua were commissioned to bring the Jews out of captivity and into the Promised Land. Judges were sent to help overcome repeated oppression. Kings were anointed with wisdom and power time after time. Whenever the Jews drifted into sin, our Lord sent prophets to warn, rebuke, and redirect them. Leaders were God's answer to the needs of His people.

In the New Testament, we are told that apostles, prophets, evangelists, pastors, and teachers are given to the Body of Christ to equip her and bring her to maturity (Eph. 4:11-13). These leaders are referred to as "gifts." Gifts are something we give to express love. It is with this understanding that we must see leaders as God's gifts to humanity. It is by God's design and will that men and women, full of the Holy Spirit, step to the forefront and lead the way for God's people.

Often Christians emphasize the fact that the Holy Spirit leads and ministers to each and every believer. This, of course, is true, and every Christian is a priest unto God, responsible for his own decisions in life. However, this cannot be stressed to the exclusion of God working through chosen vessels to lead His people.

It is the same Holy Spirit who guides and ministers to the individual believer who also raises men and women to stand at the forefront. When the Spirit of God comes upon a person, typically that individual rises from among those standing idly around and becomes salt to the earth, a city set on a hill, baptized with boldness. The Holy Spirit takes a fisherman such as Peter, lifts him from his secluded lifestyle, and plants him in downtown Jerusalem, where he fearlessly preaches to the multitudes (Acts 2:1-14). The Spirit speaks to leaders such as Paul and Barnabas, sending them forth to preach to all the nations (Acts 13:1-2). Throughout history, God, by His Spirit, has anointed individuals with great boldness to proclaim His message, purpose, and plans. In every generation, we are told, the Holy Spirit causes men and women, young ones and old ones, rich and poor, to rise and prophesy as bold witnesses of Himself and His Word (Acts 2:17-18).

No person can be an effective leader until he has settled these issues in his heart, mind, and emotions. If a person questions within himself whether or not God even wants leaders, he will not yield to the call of God. Every time he steps forward to do what he believes needs to be done, he will have pressures trying to force him to "get back among the ranks." If a person is unsure whether or not the Holy Spirit, indeed, grants authority, boldness, and wisdom, he always will be unsure of the true anointing for leadership.

Without an understanding of how the Spirit works, potential leaders will remain riddled with guilt feelings. Doubts will torment their minds every time they step out: "Should I be doing this?" "Who gave me the right to be so bold?" "I do not want to draw attention to myself!" Hesitations persist. Doubts prevail at every decision. Confidence, in the face of persecution and trials, is undermined. Every time someone comes to challenge his leadership, he cowers and shrinks back. Satan finds a foothold in doubt and, hence, robs the world of another leader. Until a man or woman decides that God actually desires, gives, and makes leaders, they never will allow the Spirit to so function through them in this capacity.

Every authority that exists is established by God (Rom. 13:1). He is the One who appoints leaders to rise. He is the One who exalts some people and holds others down in a low estate. His Word lays forth principles establishing elders and exhorting Christians to submit to their spiritual leaders (I Peter 5:1-5). The Bible is the book which tells us that it is a good thing to desire the "greater gifts" (I Cor. 12:31) and aspire to leadership within the Church (I Tim. 3:1).

God is for leadership. If you are a leader, you must know this! What you *believe* will *hinder* or *activate* your own gifts and authority. The double-minded man is unstable in all of his ways and should not expect to receive anything from the Lord (James 1:6-8). Answer the question: "Does God want and use leaders?" The truth is that *God likes leaders.* If you are a leader, then *tell yourself* that you are a leader. If you are a leader, then settle these issues within your heart and mind now.

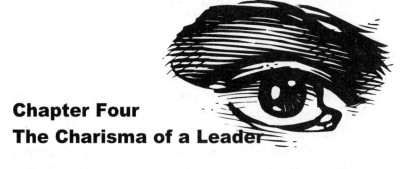

Chapter Four
The Charisma of a Leader

When a leader walks into a room, people can sense it. Another person who has no leadership qualities could walk into the same room and no one would notice. People feel drawn to look, listen, and respond to leaders. When a leader speaks, people tend to weigh his words carefully. Every leader carries an authority that can be observed.

What is it that creates such influence upon those around a leader? Charisma—the force of attraction and authority embodied in a leader. In this chapter, I want to explain this unseen force necessary for effective leadership.

Some Christians have a negative attitude about charisma. In later chapters, I will explain how evil forces can be released through the wrong use of leadership authority, but here I want to focus on true charisma, which can be used for good.

Men and women of God in the Bible had charisma. Some of them were quiet, timid individuals until the Spirit of God came upon them, enabling them boldly to lead people. Jesus had so much charisma that the established religious leaders feared Him, noting that He spoke with authority (Matt. 7:29), and in their minds, He was leading the multitudes astray. Leaders throughout Church history have possessed and used leadership abilities to direct the masses according to the purposes of God.

To understand what charisma is, we must identify how God made us. The Bible tells us that every person has three parts: a body, a soul, and a spirit (I Thess. 5:23). The body is the physical vessel which can be seen and touched. The spirit is the energy which gives life. And the soul is the created element which stands between the body and spirit.*

The spirit within all humans originated with the breath that God first breathed into Adam (Gen. 2:7; Eccl. 12:7). Just as God's words spoken at Creation, "Let the earth bring forth living creatures..." (Gen. 1:24), had enough power to produce life in animals for years to follow, so also there was enough power in that breath released into Adam to energize every human being in all the generations to follow. The spiritual energy is what enables people to live and function. We think of it as the life-force within a person.

Some Christians hesitate in using words such as "force" or "energy," because these terms are often associated with mystical or occult views. However, there is, indeed, an energy resident within every human being. The New Testament uses the Greek word *pneuma,* translated "breath" or "spirit." The best words we have today to describe accurately that biblical reality are "spiritual energy." It originated with the breath of God. That breath energizes the body.

All human beings have spiritual energy within them. The Bible tells us that if God were to pull back

*For further study on the body, soul, and spirit, see the author's book, Volume 2, in the *Spiritual Realities Series.* Information on how to obtain this is in the Appendix.

His breath from us, every person would return to dust (Job 34:14-15). Every human being, Christian and non-Christian, depends upon the spiritual life within him to remain alive.

As the spiritual energy within a person flows, the soul acts as a channel through which the spiritual energy comes forth. When one's soul is aligned with and in agreement with his spirit, the spiritual force from within is strong. If a person is confused, timid, and doubtful, these characteristics cloud the soul and act as a blocking of the energy within.

These principles are true for both the Christian and the non-Christian. However, the Christian has the added benefit of the Holy Spirit. The Bible tells us that "the one who joins himself to the Lord is one spirit with Him" (I Cor. 6:17). The spirit within the Christian is quickened by the Holy Spirit and has access to God. Therefore, the more the Christian's soul functions as an open channel, through the strength of faith, the more the Holy Spirit flows out from his innermost being (John 7:38).

In the next chapter, I will discuss how the leader can develop the proper attitude of soul which releases this spiritual energy. In this chapter, let us understand what this release of spiritual life accomplishes for a person.

First of all, we are taught in the Bible that the spirit within a person enables him not only to be alive, but also to think and make decisions. The Apostle Paul explained that the spirit of a person reveals the thoughts of that person (I Cor. 2:11). As the spiritual energy within a person flows out, it allows him to think clearly. If the spiritual flow within a person is weak, then he will have a difficult time making decisions. He will not be as sharp. In this function, the spirit is like a flashlight, illuminating the soul and revealing to a person his own thoughts.

A second function of the spirit is to enable the life of a person to flow out with words. Words are not just sound waves traveling from one person's mouth to another's ears. It is spiritual substance which gives people authority as they speak. Jesus Himself told us that His words were spirit and life (John 6:63). There is a real substance transmitted between people as they communicate. The greater the authority of the speaker, the more substance there is in his words. Hence, some people seem to have "heavy, strong words," while others can say exactly the same things, but their words seem "skinny." Words carry the spiritual authority of the speaker.

A third function of a person's spirit is a presence which emanates outward and has an effect upon others. It is the Christian belief that we do not exist merely in the natural dimension. The invisible side of one's nature is just as real as one's physical body. Furthermore, the spirit of a person influences others. To see this, read the Apostle Paul's words in the Bible concerning how Christians are bonded together in spirit; when one part of the Body hurts, we all hurt (I Cor. 12:12-27). Such Scriptures imply that our spirits are influenced by one another. This is true not just for Christians, but to some degree with all people.*

---

* For further study concerning this spiritual influence, read the author's books, Volumes 4 and 5, in the *Spiritual Realities Series.*

The presence of a person affects the thoughts of others. For example, if your father walked into the room where you are right now, you would have certain thoughts come into your mind. If your pastor walked in, different concerns and ideas would arise. And if your child came up to you, you would have entirely different emotions and thoughts triggered within you. The thoughts that become stimulated within you are influenced by the people with whom you have contact. As I mentioned earlier, if a leader of great authority walked into the room, people would turn to look. This is because authority is something that can be felt and it influences the people around it.

As we continue, we will see the significance of this flowing spiritual energy. Understand at this point that all human beings have a spirit. The spirit within the Christian, however, has been made alive by the redemptive power of God. When the Christian releases the spiritual energy within, it comes forth as rivers of living water. Therefore, the Christian should endeavor to see a full release from his innermost being. Then he will have quickened thought processes, greater authority with words, and a presence which influences this world according to the will of God.

Chapter Five
A Leader's Poise of Soul

Charisma is the result of spiritual energy resident within a person's innermost being. That spiritual energy flows out when there is an agreement between one's soul and spirit.

Agreement of soul and spirit is a quality both given and developed. Some people are born with a certain confidence. They are not swayed easily by other's opinions or views. Their souls are fixed and their spirits emanate great energy. Just as some people genetically inherit physically strong bodies, so also, some people possess spiritual strength from birth.

Others develop strength of character through experience and training. When an individual goes through stressful situations in life, he is forced to establish with more clarity what he believes. The more challenges that come against a person's belief system and patterns of thought, the more he must develop the firmness to hold to his convictions. However, reaffirming of one's beliefs and patterns of thought need not always come through trials. Education, repeated application, and associating with people of like faith also strengthen a person within.

A leader has not only strength of soul, but also what I call "the leadership poise of soul." Let's identify

25

three characteristics which determine this poise of soul.

First, a leader's life is "pointed" in a definite direction. He has determination and focus. He has a vision of where he wants to go or what he desires to accomplish. A leader can be a leader only if he knows where to point other people.

The purpose within a person can be sensed by others. Directionless people do not challenge others, and they have little influence upon those around them. The focused soul that acts as a channel. When a leader speaks according to the vision he has, spiritual energy emanates outward, stirring others to join. When a leader acts, others fall into line accordingly.

A second element evident in the poise of a leader's soul is a sense of responsibility. It is not enough for a person merely to believe something strongly or simply want to see it accomplished. Only if one accepts personal responsibility will he activate the quality we know as leadership.

To visualize this, picture a classroom of young students waiting for their teacher to arrive. When the experienced teacher walks into the room, the students immediately will quiet down and prepare to receive instructions. The teacher walks into the room carrying authority because he or she holds responsibility for that classroom. If, on the other hand, a substitute teacher (who is there just for the day's wage) walks into the same room, the students will not respond with anywhere near the same respect. The students can sense whether the teacher, indeed, has authority over the classroom.

When one individual *accepts* responsibility, it causes others to *yield* responsibility and, hence, give authority. To the degree responsibility is accepted, authority is given.

Furthermore, a sense of responsibility is a force which molds within a person the characteristics necessary for leadership. For this reason, a child who is reared carrying the responsibility of helping with siblings is more likely to grow up to be a leader. A person put in charge of overseeing great works that include many people, gradually is molded into the required vessel. The sense of responsibility trains a person to be conscious of the bigger picture and longer-range goals. It positions the soul in a way that releases the energy which others can sense and to which they can respond.

The last element—which is of key importance in the poise of a leader's soul—is "detachment." By detachment, I mean a sense wherein the leader remains above circumstances, entanglements, and problems. The Bible calls church leaders "overseers," referring to their role of "seeing over" their areas of responsibility. The leader must remain a little bit removed from the situations of life into which others would be pulled. As an eagle flying high above can see a broad area below, so also a leader must maintain a distinct, separated perspective in order to maintain the ability to see the "big picture." If he loses this detachment and becomes too involved, he will lose the proper poise of soul necessary for leadership influence to continue.

Detachment is accomplished in different ways by various leaders. Some develop a sports activity or hobby, separate from their work, through which they can escape the ongoing pressures which all too easily can pull them in and under. Other leaders use humor in a way that releases tension and allows them to step out of the seriousness of their work. Others write books, which gives them a more objective view, or they read novels that temporarily remove them from the real world. Some leaders are able to remain detached from their work through prayer and by retreating into a relationship with God.

Often detachment is misunderstood by those following a strong leader. They sometimes perceive the leader as distant or uncaring. Of course, this is not to make excuses for a negligent leader, but detachment must be accepted and understood as an essential element. The wise leader will recognize this, but he also will recognize the tendency in people to misunderstand this poise of soul.

To help avoid such misunderstandings, a leader can make extra effort to communicate love and care for those involved. It does little good to explain only the *logic* of it to one's followers, because what they deal with is of the *heart*, that is, emotions related to distance and aloneness. A leader must not be removed so far from people that they feel abandoned. He must never be elevated to a place where people feel degraded or insignificant. *Two steps* ahead and a leader will lose people. *No steps* ahead and he will lose the ability to point the way. *One step* ahead—with constant communication from the heart—and others will follow.

It is the poise of soul that enables a leader to lead.

Vision and purpose focus one's attention so he will not be side-tracked easily into concerns which would deter from the goal. The sense of responsibility opens a person's eyes to see the needs of others and what must be done to accomplish the tasks at hand. Detachment enables a leader to keep perspective for objective decisions in view of long-range goals. Purpose, a sense of responsibility, and detachment all work together to position the soul of a leader properly.

With the soul positioned and focused, spiritual energy flows out accordingly. This energy stimulates progress, stirs others to join in, opens doors, and influences circumstances. It is spiritual energy which emanates outward to accomplish the necessary work.

As we explained in the last chapter, spiritual energy (when released) floods the soul of the leader, opening his eyes to see what must be done each step of the way. The spirit within a person reveals the thoughts of that person (I Cor. 2:11). When the spirit is not activated and freely flowing outward, then a person's thoughts are clouded. He cannot make decisions easily. However, when spiritual energy is allowed to emanate outward, the soul is illuminated as a dark room filled with light. An eye-opening occurs. Ideas are born. Thoughts align. Answers form. Direction is given. Decisions are made.

It is important to understand that poise of soul brings the answers that leaders need. *Do not reverse this order in your mind.* Leaders are not leaders because they have answers. They have answers and ideas because they have accepted responsibility and maintain proper detachment.

Of course, training and experience are essential. People quickly sense if a certain leader knows what he is talking about. Yet, they also expect the leader to be on top, in charge, and fully capable. In the comparison I made with an eagle flying high, the eagle can see more because of its position. So, also, direction and answers come to a leader because his soul is positioned correctly. If a leader loses the poise of soul which is so vital, he loses authority and the ability to lead. If he maintains focus of soul, he will remain in the place where inspired thoughts come and solutions formulate. Answers are the result of soul poise. Leadership is the fruit.

Maintaining soul poise requires an output of energy. It is not for the lazy or uncaring. In the face of trials and persecution, it would be easier for the leader to let go or shrink back from responsibilities. The tendency is to lose poise of soul. When opponents come, the leader must stand his ground and remain strong. Others will test the leader to see if he is worth following. Strength of character (a desirable trait) must not be confused with stubbornness or an unwillingness to listen to others; however, neither should it be used in that way. I am not making an excuse for that. But we must recognize that being a leader is work.

Train a person how to poise his soul and you have helped him become a leader. He is more likely to have answers and be able to make decisions. There will be a presence that others can sense. People will yield to his vision and direction. Teach a pastor how to stand before his people, and they will recognize the call from

God. Instruct a classroom teacher how to position his soul, and he will maintain authority over the students. Show a father how to accept responsibility for his family, and he will win the respect of his family. Help a politician become detached and goal-oriented, and he will be able to govern the people. Train a businessperson how to position over his business, and he will be more efficient and effective in running that business. Leaders are both born and made!

Chapter Six
Beyond Authority Limits

We have identified the soul of a leader as one which releases spiritual energy. Now let's study the importance of exercising authority *only* over that which God has ordained. Whenever a person, Christian or non-Christian, poises his soul over that which is not under his authority, evil energies may be released. It is this wrong use of authority, or the usurping of authority, which we now will examine.

It is important to realize that every poised soul receives ideas concerning how to govern. To see this, picture someone watching a football game. They either can sit back and enjoy, or they can poise themselves over everything going on out on the field. If they poise themselves over the game, they will start analyzing, developing a strategy of their own, and even begin noting when the coach could have made better decisions.

Similarly, we see ideas coming into the mind of the person poising their soul over another person's work in the home. For example, if you go to your neighbor's house so they can cook dinner for you, you either can observe casually, or you can poise your soul over all the work being done in the kitchen. If you poise your soul in that fashion, you will begin seeing the cook's mistakes, and thoughts will come into your mind as to how things could be done more efficiently or somehow better. As every cook knows, it is not very much fun having someone looking over your shoulder "advising" you.

These principles work in all areas of life. The poised soul is an open channel for spiritual energy to flood the mind.

Now picture a typical church with about 120 people attending. As the appointed leader, Pastor Bill has goals for the congregation. For every service, he tries to have a message which will advance the people in the specific direction he believes God is leading. However, there is an older gentleman named George in this church, and George thinks the direction of the Lord is completely different. George has been a member of the church for a long time and because the people respect his judgment, he feels responsible for them to some degree. Because of his disagreement with Pastor Bill, George has been very upset lately.

Every Sunday morning George sits among the congregation critically examining whatever is going on. All week long George cannot keep from thinking about the direction he is convinced the church should be going. He even prays daily for God to change Pastor Bill. Week after week, there George sits, carrying a sense of responsibility and detachment, with thoughts becoming more and more fixed.

What is happening spiritually? George is releasing spiritual forces. Not only is he formulating his own ideas, but the spiritual energy within George emanates outward, having a very real effect upon the congregation. Whenever Pastor Bill makes a strong point, people sitting around George glance over at him to see what his reactions are. With a slightly raised eyebrow or a frown, George passes judgment and undermines what Pastor Bill is attempting to accomplish. As George's soul is poised, the people will be supernaturally manipulated to yield responsibility and, hence, give authority to George. They will become more and more aware of George's reactions to whatever is being said. Even though he may say nothing audibly, the people will be strongly influenced by his beliefs.

Pastor Bill also will be influenced. Emanating out of George are energies which actually bombard Pastor Bill as he speaks, thinks, and tries to make decisions. George's spiritual energies work against Pastor Bill, weakening him and hindering him as he tries to progress toward his goals. George is partially binding the anointing and the flow of the Holy Spirit through the pastor.

Even though George is not in front preaching from the pulpit, he is *usurping authority* over the church. We already stated that in this example Pastor Bill is the appointed leader. If, indeed, God has placed Bill in that position, then what George is doing is wrong. The ideas that George is receiving are not from God, because God's ideas come through God-given authority. A person whose soul is poised over some ministry may receive direction and information that sounds spiritual, biblical, and godly, but those ideas always will be tainted in some way, if the authority has been usurped wrongly. By poising his soul, George is taking authority that God has not given to him. Whether or not he realizes it, George is releasing negative energies. Even though George is praying and thinks he is doing God's will, he is an open channel which the devil can use to destroy.

I am not saying that it is always wrong for a congregational member to come against a leader. There have been times throughout Church history in which advancements only came because someone took a bold stand against established Church leadership. There is a time when the Holy Spirit may come upon an individual and anoint him or her to challenge and confront evil, even if it is among leaders (Job 32:1-10).

More commonly though, a person in a position of lesser authority should pray for his leaders and speak respectfully to them. God should be trusted for any needed changes. Paul wrote to Timothy that he should not rebuke any elder, but rather, appeal to him as to a father (I Tim. 5:1). Leaders can make mistakes, but still we must deal with them in a fashion honoring their God-given authority.

In our example of George and Pastor Bill, we saw George taking authority by an act of his own will. This is wrong. What an individual does by poising his soul in the authority position is identical to what witches do in controlling and manipulating others. Therefore, we often label such exercises as "witchcraft," even if they are done by Christians. Every leader must poise his soul. But to poise it over an area that God has not given to you is violating another's authority, and it must be recognized as an open door for evil.

Intercessors and prayer warriors sometimes fall into a similar misuse of power. Take, for example, a group of three or four sincere Christians who meet weekly to pray and fast for the church and its leaders. Such prayer is of great benefit when done correctly, but untrained people may pray in a way that poises their soul "over" their leaders. When a group of intercessors starts taking responsibility for the guidance and direction of their minister, they can cause problems, actually binding or hindering his anointing in some way. In prayer, they may take on a detached, purposeful poise of soul and elevate themselves above the one for whom they are praying. When they become united in their thoughts and requests, they increase tremendously the forces flowing through them. In addition, fasting, e.g., going without any food for a time, focuses the soul so that it acts as a clearer channel for spiritual energy. If all that energy is directed upon the leader, or in a direction contrary to where he feels led to go, he will feel bombarded, oppressed, confused, attacked, defeated, etc. Misguided prayers hinder, rather than help leaders. Demonic powers sometimes are released and this, too, is a form of witchcraft.

The proper role of intercessors is to *undergird* and *uplift* their leaders. There may be a temporary period during which they "cover" their leaders with prayer, because trials and spiritual attacks seem to be too strong, but in general, they are to position themselves in respect to authority, "beneath" their leaders. When the Apostle Paul asked for prayer, he requested the believers to beseech God that he might have greater boldness, open doors, and protection. Notice, they were to pray for his success, rather than try to *put their thoughts and desires upon him.* Prayers for a leader should be directed toward giving him strength and power to fulfill the leading of the Spirit that he receives. In other words, they must elevate their leaders; the leader must increase and they must decrease. Praying in this fashion recognizes and builds authority, rather than suppressing it. Therefore, I prefer to teach about "prayer support" or "prayer shields," rather than "prayer coverings."

There are some teachings and works in the Body of Christ today which actually promote wrong relationships between leaders and those they are called to lead. We must warn against these.

For example, some Christians have heard a teaching about being "a watchman on the tower." They take this terminology and begin to think of themselves as watchmen over the church which they attend. Of course, it is important for every Christian to know God's leading for their individual lives, and they do have personal responsibility to verify that what their leaders are teaching, is, in fact, biblically accurate. However, when a person thinks of himself as "on the tower," he has detached and positioned above everyone else. When he claims to be a "watchman," he is claiming God-given responsibility for that specific work. A "watchman-on-the-tower-attitude" is the poise of soul against which I have been warning you and declaring as wrong—unless, of course, God, indeed, has placed a person in that position of authority.

Look with the same understanding at the destruction which can come to a church through flattery. Picture a church in which a well-known, respected minister comes to speak for one meeting. At the end of that meeting, let's say this minister points to two members in the congregation and says to one, "You have a gift of discernment and you know the appointed times for this church," and then to the other he says, "You have authority which is being denied and you need to rise up and govern." All too often I have seen that such statements over individuals' lives are misunderstood and eventually lead to destruction. Though the words may have been meant for encouragement, the two individuals may respond by poising themselves over their church, ultimately disrupting the authority which God already had established.

In my own ministry, I travel and speak in churches of many denominations and doctrinal persuasions. It is easy, therefore, to see on a large scale the results of spiritual energies being released in individual churches. I believe that evil practices involving these forces hurt and destroy more churches than any other single element. Of course, we could talk simply about our carnal nature and sinfulness as being the worst evil, but our focus here is on the oppression that comes upon leaders through others wrongfully poising their souls, leading to tremendous power struggles. Leaders under the pressure of these released evil forces have a difficult time determining God's leading, making decisions, and being bold. The spiritual flow from within them is pushed back and hindered as others reject their influence. More Christian leaders succumb to this type of spiritual pressure than to sexual sins, lust for possessions, deceptions, or other attacks of the enemy—although any of these evils may fall upon the leader who already is discouraged and weakened due to the forces of such witchcraft.

It is time for Christians to learn these principles of authority and how spiritual energies flow. Disrupting the ongoing work of God's people leaves devastation in many, many lives. The health of the church is dependent upon the proper flow of God's Spirit. What we loose is loosed and what we bind is bound. The poised soul is a weapon that can be used for or against God's Kingdom.

These issues are critical. In the next chapter, I will discuss how a leader called of God can deal with a person who is rising and challenging his authority.

Chapter Seven
Power Struggles

Several years ago I heard Dr. David Yonggi Cho give an interesting talk about the challenges of his ministry. At that time Dr. Cho had the largest church in the world, numbering over half a million people. He explained that the most difficult trials were not those involving financial stress nor dealing with the tremendous numbers of people. Rather, it was conflicts with his own elders. Dr. Cho testified that throughout the years of growth, leaders among his own team would repeatedly rise and try to assert their own authority, declaring that they had the leading of the Lord. Each time he had to meet the challenge and battle for his own position as head of the church over which God had positioned him.

Power struggles. No leader can be involved in ministry for very long and not be confronted. Understanding such conflicts can ensure that the victory will be our Lord's, while pain will be minimized.

As we discuss this, we will focus upon leadership within a church. You will notice that I portray the proper structure of the local church as consisting of several elders sharing the oversight of a congregation, but one leader standing out among the elders as the senior minister, providing the overall vision and direction. Of course, some churches are structured differently, with no elders nor designated leader at the forefront. I have explained in another book, *The Complete Wineskin,* why those forms of church government are deficient and will not experience the greatest blessings of God. In this book, I continue by assuming and describing the structure of a church as consisting of one senior minister, called by God to direct a congregation, with several elders sharing the responsibility, but still under the senior minister.

In power struggles, the people typically used to challenge authority in any serious way are neither ignorant nor young, inexperienced Christians. On the contrary, those who assert themselves wrongly are usually Christians already respected in the religious community. Of course, there may be young, overzealous ones involved in spurts of anger or temporary periods of controversy, but the ones causing serious difficulties are typically those who are long-standing church members and, therefore, who have much experience and some authority.

Look at the Jewish nation and those who rose up against Moses (Num. 16). It was not the unknown, untrained rebels who held no position among the people. We are told that Korah led 250 leaders of the congregation to step out against Moses. These men were described as "chosen in the assembly, men of renown" (Num. 16:2). They began grumbling against Moses' leadership, and they reasoned that they could hear God as well as Moses could. Those who rose up in this rebellion were Levites—religious leaders, respected men who were trained in the things of God.

In similar fashion, we see in the Church today that those commonly used in such authority-challenging power struggles are people who themselves have religious training, experience, and the respect of the people. It is these co-workers and co-leaders who sometimes end up in conflict with the senior minister: elders, worship leaders, youth pastors, Bible study leaders, those who have some Bible school training, long-standing members of the congregation, or spouses of the same.

When a strong individual disagrees with an area in the senior minister's life, he may start meditating on what should be corrected and how things could be better. Soon the dissatisfied one is detached and formulating ideas on how things should be run. The devil can take advantage of those thought processes and feed in his own thoughts, giving rise to a very critical attitude. Then a few other people can be pulled easily into the same negative ways of thinking. If they begin to feel responsible to correct the errors which they see, they soon will be poised over all that is happening.

As I explain how the leader is to deal with such a situation, some readers may want me to address the other side of the issue. What should congregational members do when the key leaders are in obvious error? Most people have times serving on both sides of the fence. Is there anything that the sheep can do to keep the shepherd on the right path?

I will not examine this issue in depth here because my purpose in this book is to train leaders, but I can reassure those under a misguided leader that their most effective tool is prayer. Those prayers must not be directed as a spiritual force "toward" or "over" the leader, however, anyone can and should pray to God *for* their leader (I Tim. 2:1-3). There are also times that direct confrontation is necessary and appropriate. Paul confronted Peter when Peter was being two-faced about his stand on Gentile Christians (Gal. 2:11).

A person also has the option of leaving. No one should stay involved, feigning support for a leader who continues in sin for any length of time. What *is* wrong, against which people should be warned, is gossip, poising one's soul over the leader, or gathering a group of dissidents.

Having stated that, let's turn our attention back to the leader himself. What is the appropriate response when his authority is challenged?

If we go back to read about Moses and Korah, the first thing we learn that Moses did was this: "he fell on his face" (Num. 16:4). This is the starting point. Before a leader defends his position, he must hear from God that, indeed, he is in the right position. He needs to analyze his own life to see where he has erred. No one can remove the speck from another's eye until he has taken the log out of his own eye.

One of the most common mistakes senior ministers make in facing people such as Korah is in not realizing that they themselves as the leader may have given Korah place—in fact, created him. This error usually is made if and when the senior minister yields the authority of the local church for a time and allows some other person to embrace it. For example, if a senior minister leaves his church for a month or two, someone else must be left in charge. No one truly can take charge without rising and posturing themselves in a position of authority over the church. They really cannot receive inspired teachings, nor govern effectively, unless they themselves rise. Therefore, it is expected of them. Then when a senior minister returns from a missions trip, or a vacation, or any other break, he must realize that someone may have stepped into his position. It is a spiritual position which is not released easily. Furthermore, the people will tend to yield to such temporary leadership. That is how leadership dynamics work. Entirely new authority dynamics can be established in a church in a relatively brief period.

What is a senior minister to do if he returns to a congregation and finds this to be the case? First of all, he must realize the error. He made a mistake. Compare it with a father relinquishing his child to the care of a foster-parent. That father would be foolish to think that he could return at any time and take the child back without some deep, emotional wounds happening in both the fosterparent and the child. A bond has formed and breaking that bond will have hurtful consequences.

If a senior minister realizes that he, indeed, abandoned the position of caring for the flock and another rose up to take it, he should decide before God whether or not to take back the leadership position. It is not a "hireling position" but a position of love and responsibility. If the senior minister yielded the position to another temporarily, he may decide that it is best to give it away permanently. As the two women who fought over the ownership of a child before King Solomon, so also two leaders may battle for the care of a flock. When Solomon said, "Divide the living child in two, and give half to the one and half to the other," the real mother cried out to give the living child to the false mother (I Kings 3:24-26). Solomon knew from that response that the true mother was the one willing to give it away, and so he gave the child to the true mother. In similar fashion, there are times when a senior minister will offer to give away his child—the flock—lest they be cut in two. I have seen in such cases that, indeed, God will act as Solomon did, and someday in the future—maybe years down the road—the flock and the new leader will recognize the love of their first pastor and, therefore, honor him.

On the other hand, if the senior minister stands up and demands his position back, the flock typically is cut in two. Now, in a minute we will talk about a time when even that is necessary and how the senior minister can minimize the damages. However, first we must finish dealing with the senior minister's heart. Did he, indeed, yield the place of responsibility to another? If so, he needs to repent before God.

Of course, there also can be other errors made by the senior minister which may have caused the division. In Chapter Nine we will discuss *relational adultery,* which frequently is at the heart of church splits. In addition to that sin, a senior minister must look into his own heart and see if he has been faithful to God for the ministry to which God has called him.

Analyzing one's own heart is difficult, if not impossible. We too easily can deceive ourselves. Therefore, we need to trust other people to walk alongside of us. Every leader needs some other leaders in whom he can trust to encourage and, when necessary, confront him. When power struggles are taking place in a local church, outside advice is especially helpful.

Assuming a senior minister has gone before God and other trusted leaders, what is he to do next if someone is challenging his place in leadership? If the leader has decided before God that he is not to "give up the child," but, indeed, fight for it, he must, above all else, *remain composed.*

Let me restate that: Do not lose composure.

One more time: Stay composed.

King Solomon tells us in Ecclesiastes 10:4, "...composure allays great offenses." Do you want offenses laid at rest? Then stay composed.

In such a situation, a leader must be as a shock absorber. On a car there are shock absorbers so that when the automobile drives over a rough spot on the road, the shock is absorbed and the rest of the car remains stable, riding smoothly. Likewise, a leader must be able to absorb the shock of other peoples' frustration, accusations, and even carnality. In the face of someone who is unloading their complaint angrily, the leader must be stable, still, anchored in God. Even if his own emotions are raging, the leader will be wise to stay composed on the outside. The leader must not get defensive. Even when people are making groundless accusations, he will be wise to listen carefully and hold his response until the appropriate time.

In the long run, people will measure a leader, not by the accusations, but by how he reacts to the accusations.

The leader's *presence* will determine the outcome. Therefore, a leader should sit confidently and lovingly in the presence of those who have complaints. He needs to listen and remain secure. His presence is the most powerful force he possesses to bring peace and reassure others.

Even Korah, the person most responsible for causing an uprising, usually can be won back if the senior minister will stay composed. In his composure, the leader must not see Korah as an enemy. If the senior minister acts defensively or decides that he is going to destroy Korah, he also will destroy part of the church. It is almost impossible to remove a co-leader in a church without removing the portion of the church that has grown to trust and love that co-leader. The wise senior minister does everything possible to try to "win back" that co-leader. This is not only for the sake of the people, but for the sake of the co-leader. Usually that co-leader is a person who has walked with the senior minister for some time. Leaders don't throw away other leaders that easily.

I learned a powerful lesson when I watched a very successful leader deal with his associate pastor, who had walked out on him in disillusionment and anger. That leader did not allow negative thoughts to flood his mind, such as, "Oh, he was too much trouble anyway," or "It would not be worth the work of going after him." Instead, he confidently decided to win back his co-worker, friend, and disciple. He looked at the relationship as a life-long ministry partnership, not as binding as marriage, but still serious. He had no hesitations in pursuing his disgruntled disciple, and, indeed, he did win him back. Successful leaders do that. They think in terms of lifelong relationships. If you think this way will you minimize power struggles. Ministers who develop large ministries do not give up easily. Nor do they tolerate negative ideas about their co-workers in their thoughts or speech. You will not hear a strong leader talking badly about those who work with him. Thoughts are not even entertained concerning possible breaks in relationships. If a co-leader does drift away, the mature leader goes after him. The successful leader believes that he can win back the straying individual. He becomes a sounding board and even a shock absorber for the disgruntled individual. The leader remains secure when all of this is occurring.

Composure is much the same as the poise of soul which I discussed earlier. If a leader, ordained by God, keeps soul poise, he releases the Spirit of God. The authority of God begins to put things in order and actively work upon circumstances and people who are in opposition. The Spirit also floods the soul of the leader, quickening his mind and inspiring thoughts. In the face of conflict, therefore, the leader will have continuous revelation concerning what must be done, and when. The Holy Spirit provides solutions and tells the leader to whom he should talk and what should be said. God works both within and outside the leader if he keeps the channel of his soul open.

How, then, can the leader remain an open channel? As we discussed earlier, he must remain detached. He must not allow himself to get pulled so far into a fight (or under fear, or into confusion) that he loses the leadership perspective. It is for this reason that some of the most powerful leaders alive, in the face of the most intense pressure, tell a few jokes, go fishing, or play a game of golf. Napoleon, before going into his greatest battles, was known to take a short nap. At the most critical moment of one of the largest church splits that ever happened in America, the key leader went into his office, put his feet up, and confidently said, "Everything is going to work out." It was precisely that attitude of knowing and understanding authority that allowed him to advance to that position of authority in the first place. Detachment means keeping a bird's-eye perspective at all times.

In emphasizing detachment, I do not want to make a leader appear uninterested or not emotionally involved. Of course, division and conflict hurts. Every leader will experience pain—sometimes intense—when those he oversees go through difficulties. The detachment of which we speak is a confidence in God that all things will work out for His glory.

To maintain poise of soul, the leader also must hold a sense of responsibility. He cannot surrender it to anyone else. The senior leader must not allow anyone to grasp the responsibility of providing the overall vision and direction. If the leader maintains responsibility, no one can grab the authority. This is how to win in a power struggle.

Finally, if the battle goes on and the straying individual cannot be won, the leader may have to ask—even insist—that Korah leave the flock. This is sad. This is difficult. This is the last means of dealing with the situation. Do it firmly, with empathy and composure, but without guilt.

Chapter Eight
Keeping Peace

More important than winning in power struggles is avoiding them altogether. The wise leader will accomplish this by teaching his co-leaders the principles of authority we have been discussing. There are also practical steps he can take to avoid power struggles and keep peace reigning throughout an organization or church.

In the previous chapter, we talked about the minister who temporarily left his church in the hands of another leader. We saw how such a situation can lead to problems. Now, let's mention some precautions that can be taken to avoid such difficulties from even taking root.

A senior minister who decides to leave his church for any length of time should, first of all, give the oversight to someone he can trust. Second, the leader needs to talk openly with that trusted person about not taking "ownership" of the church. If and when a senior minister is gone for a time, it is good to keep his name before the congregation. Every Sunday service, the temporary leader should report what the senior minister is doing. On occasion, a letter or note from the senior minister should be read to the people. Communication must continue. Most important, the senior person must hold in his heart the people for whom God has given him responsibility (this will be explained more fully in Chapter 12).

Another situation in which power struggles frequently develop is a few months (usually about nine months) after a new minister takes over the leadership of a church. At first, everyone usually loves the new minister. But sooner or later—when he tries to introduce changes—battles begin. How can these problems be avoided?

It is helpful to recognize the authority dynamics which become established in a church while there is no leader. During the period between one minister leaving and a new one taking over, someone or several people will begin carrying certain responsibilities. It is not the people who carry the servant responsibilities, such as cleaning the toilets or running the PA, who later cause problems, but the individuals who had to care for the younger Christians or who kept the church going financially. It is they who had to rise into the place of responsibility for the people. They were required to poise themselves in a position of authority. Turning that position over to a new minister is not always easy.

In explaining this, I do not want to side with the incoming minister nor the old-time members holding responsibility. I simply want us to recognize the dynamics of authority. An incoming minister is naive to think that he can take everything over in just a matter of days or weeks. It may happen on the legal documents, but the hearts of people and the mantle of authority move slower. The wise leader realizes this.

Many churches have established a policy that

when a new senior minister takes over, everyone previously holding a position of authority is asked to step down. Then the new minister is given time to put into those positions the people with whom he feels comfortable. This is a good practice, however, it still involves pain. People required to step down often have years of their own lives invested in the work. They care for the people. Rarely does an incoming minister realize the great investment that has been made by various congregational members. Still, it is a good practice, and I believe that an incoming minister should insist on this privilege of choosing his own staff. However, he should help the previous workers make the necessary changes and repeatedly express concern for them. Those co-leaders may even have to go through a period of mourning. It is natural. It is healthy and should be encouraged. It would be un-Christian and uncaring for an incoming minister to deny those individuals a reasonable time to make the necessary transition.

If a new minister comes into a new church as "a bull in a china closet," many people will be hurt. He may rationalize an aggressive takeover in his own mind, but it is not necessary and it is not right.

Time and patience are required. The hearts of people take time to turn. Confidence and respect is *earned*. I caution young ministers from being too eager to trash the past and forge ahead too quickly.

Of course, there will be some whose hearts are never able to embrace the new leader. There also will be a few who never could be satisfied by anything the new minister does. And finally, there are some things which the new minister never will do as effectively as the old one. Change necessitates change. This should not be hard to understand, but it will be for a few.

For those few, it is not changing the minister which is so hard. It is changing the color of the carpet, removing the organ which has been in the front of the sanctuary for thirty years, taking down the bulletin board, or telling Sister Suzy (who sings out of key) that she no longer can be on the worship team. The things which people have grown to identify with *their church* are sacred in their minds and hearts.

A new minister has the authority to change these things, but he needs to move slowly and confidently. There is no need to do everything immediately upon his arrival but, rather, he needs to think in terms of months and years. Still there is no doubt that change will come. Sooner or later the leader will be "tearing down the golden calves." This is life. He will need to make the church building fit. The worship style must change. In time, everything must take on the leader's nature. I even have counseled incoming ministers to take a night or two and sleep in their sanctuary, for that is a spiritual exercise which grants him more authority to preach in that very place. As a woman makes her home uniquely hers, once she moves in, so also a new leader must have the freedom and courage to make the church his.

Let's go one step further and say that the leader not only must take authority of the natural facility, but he also must grow into a poise of soul to oversee the congregation. Until he does, he will be only a hireling getting paid to do a job. Sometime during the ministry, hopefully very soon, the people must become *his* people. The leader must hurt for them and rejoice with them. He must accept responsibility before God for the welfare of their souls (Heb. 13:17). Of course, that involves a process of change and growing, but it is real.

In time, a senior minister will need to gather a staff, deacons, and elders—or whatever their church calls its co-leaders. Too often young ministers attempt to do this too early. They feel pressured to gather elders around them to confirm and add credibility to their own ministries. Young leaders must be warned not to yield to their own insecurities. Staff who are in servant positions must be recruited early on, but elders who will help carry the responsibility for overseeing the church must not be chosen right away. I like to see a senior minister work with co-leaders for at least three years before anyone is given the title "elder." It is also common for a senior minister to work with the same people for seven years before his team is formed. These time periods are not stated as a legalistic standard; it is simply that through experience with many churches, I have seen that decisions made prematurely can yield destruction down the road.

Next, it is essential that everyone involved in leadership actually is producing and working. An idle person is a detached person. As soon as an elder, deacon, or Bible-study leader (or the spouse of the same) become uninvolved in the ongoing ministry, it is easy for them to sit back and take an exclusively judicial role, rather than a role of actually ministering to the people. We need servants and shepherds, not policymakers. A judicial role, by its very nature, seats a person in a position of authority, *looking down* on the rest of the people. From there, a critical attitude can take hold all too easily. Any co-leader who is not actively working in the ministry—with the people—is a candidate for the same type of deception into which Korah fell.

In this sense, the average church today is at greater risk for strife and division than most businesses. In the secular world, businesses are structured for production, and anyone not producing is eliminated automatically. Too many churches, in contrast, are structured to be nonproductive. People are not expected to do anything more than sit, listen, and think. Such a system is a perfect environment in which to create grumbling and discontentment. Uninvolved people are detached people. A wise leader will not allow this. He structures the church for productivity. Everyone who holds authority in the church must be accomplishing something.

From experience in many churches, I can tell you that a detached elder is often a "future church-split." The only way to avoid power struggles is for the senior minister to arrange for all those involved in leadership to be working actively in the ongoing ministry. Everyone else automatically is asked to step down. Wise leaders actually write this in their by-laws and practice it. If an elder or other person with authority becomes removed from regular involvement in the church's life, due to career demands, family concerns, physical illness, long vacations, disinterest, or other things pulling them away, then they automatically are expected to step down. Authority necessitates present involvement. A church cannot be governed effectively any other way.

Co-leaders do carry responsibility and authority. However, the key God-appointed leader must hold the responsibility for the overall direction and vision of the ministry. He then delegates and shares areas of responsibility to those under him. All elders, deacons, Bible-study leaders, etc., must be under the senior minister. *They should poise their souls over their individual areas of ministry,* but the head minister never must abdicate his own responsibility to oversee the overall ministry. The senior minister must establish within himself the call from God and communicate it clearly to those who serve under him.

Chapter Nine
Relational Adultery

One more topic needs to be considered when we talk about avoiding church struggles and splits. It is called *relational adultery*. This does not refer to any physical or sexual relationship between two people, but rather, a new bonding of heart which violates already established relationships.

For example, a church may be progressing successfully for some time with several leaders working together in unity and peace. But then a new person may join the congregation, a person who has some level of success, giftings, or authority. It may be a businessperson who is successful in the community, or a doctor, or a lawyer. It may be a person who was once in ministry, so they already carry a certain amount of charisma and experience related to churchwork. Or it even can be a past friend of the senior minister who comes to join the church.

The trouble begins when the senior minister opens his heart to the newcomer and welcomes him in without concern for those who already have been placed in leadership. An outsider welcomed in can—and usually does—disrupt already established relationships. Relational adultery is the result.

To see the seriousness of this, we need to realize that people work not only for money, status, or for the

Lord, but also for the privilege of being close to the senior person. This is an unspoken benefit but a very important one.

In most organizations there is even a "pecking order" established among the co-leaders. That order may or may not be written on paper, but *it is established and upheld in the heart of the senior leader*. Of course, the senior minister should hold all of his co-leaders within his own heart in a place of care and commitment. However, it is unavoidable that some individuals will be closer than others.

Once a leadership team has developed, problems easily arise when a new person is allowed to come on board, and particularly if he is allowed close to the heart of the senior person. Co-leaders may react— sometimes very assertively. They have a right to do so because they have paid a price to be in their current positions. They probably have given their time and adjusted their entire lives around the work they do. In addition, their families have had to make ongoing sacrifices. They have a right, therefore, to be treated in a respectful, valued way.

If a senior leader embraces another person in lieu of those who already are in positions, relationship violations result. As a woman who has been set aside by her husband in favor of another woman—a younger, more attractive woman—will feel violated, so also co-leaders can feel violated if the senior leader welcomes a new person in without their approval and heart embrace.

The experienced leader understands this. It is true not only in churches but teams, clubs, organizations, and businesses, as well. Relationships must be valued. Commitment and faithfulness need to be honored. It is wrong to "jerk" people around, which, indeed, happens as the key leader first allows one person and then another closer to him in relationships.

When co-leaders are being replaced, they will react. It may or may not be done openly, but in their hearts they will sense that the senior leader is moving someone else closer to his heart. As a woman may rise in hatred toward another woman who is stealing her husband's heart, so also, co-leaders may experience a rage rising within them. The unknowing senior person may be ignorant of what is happening and wrongly condemn a co-leader who acts in inappropriate ways. Indeed, the reaction of people can be irrational and exaggerated, but we need to recognize the tearing which may be occurring within their hearts. They are being cheated and the senior leader is wrong in treating them so carelessly.

Of course, there are times when new people need to be brought among the leadership and old ones replaced. We are not suggesting that change should be avoided. Rather, we simply are discussing the importance of making such changes with understanding and heart-felt concern.

At times the newcomer who moves close to the heart of the senior leader is someone who will not hold even an official position. It may be the quiet intercessor in the congregation or the person who plays golf with the minister. It even may be someone outside of the church. A minister may attend a conference in another location and bond in heart with the hosts of that conference to such a degree that his loyalty changes to them.

The newcomer may be even a new spouse. When a single leader dates, courts, or marries a person, he/she inevitably will change. There are dynamics which occur in one's heart which will adjust everything one thinks and does. Other people lose their place of significance and influence.

Speaking of marriage, it may not be a *new* spouse which rises to a place of influence. A wife who spent years caring for her younger children may decide to get more involved with her husband's work after the children are grown. She may end her career in another field, and this, too, will result in a change of positional influence in her husband's heart.

Such changes are occurring constantly. Every organization is in constant motion. Some of the greatest trials of any group are associated with those changes. Pain can be minimized simply by being aware of what is happening.

Unfortunately, the resulting pain often is greater in Christian ministries than it will be in businesses. This is because motives for involvement are usually more personal than financial. Plus, ministry is tied up with everything they believe about God, others, and themselves.

The Christian world offers spiritual concepts and vocabulary (Christian buzzwords) all its own which can be applied to the emotional pain of breaking relationships. For example, if a wife rises to stand by her husband who is the senior minister, co-workers who become displaced may accuse the wife of having a *controlling spirit* or even of being *Jezebel,* which is a term sometimes thrown around in Church circles to indicate an evil woman who manipulates her husband. A wife coming under such accusations will have to be defended assertively by her husband, and if she is not, she can be devastated emotionally.

The whole issue should be raised whether it is right for a husband and wife to share leadership together. I personally believe that the marriage relationship is more sacred than relationships among church leaders. Unity between a husband and wife is of more importance than unity among co-leaders. To keep marriages united, both husbands and wives need to be involved together to some degree in the ongoing work. Of course, there are times when one spouse may be giving most of his or her energy to the children or a separate career. In some situations that works well. However, God's purpose for marriage is that "two shall become one." There may be exceptions to this, and there may be short periods of time during which certain co-leaders seem to be completely united in their thoughts and hearts, but over the long run the marriage relationship of each should be held in a place of higher value than the relationships of co-workers and leaders. A strong church is made of strong marriages.

In conclusion, we can say that the senior leader has the power to keep peace within the organization he leads. If he commits relational adultery, co-leaders likely will feel violated, and they may be justified in those feelings. All the people under their leadership may feel as children tossed about in a family which has experienced divorce. It is not good. The wise leader values relationships.

Chapter Ten
Filling Your Metron

It is now time to turn our attention from the struggles and battles of leadership and examine the expansion of our own works. How can our present authority grow? How can we accomplish more in this life?

Metron is a Greek work used in the New Testament and usually is translated with the word "measure." In Romans 12:3 we are told that to every person is given a measure of faith. Paul used the word "metron" when writing to the Corinthians.

> *But we will not boast beyond our measure, but within the measure of the sphere which God has apportioned to us as a measure to reach even as far as you.*
>
> (II Cor. 10-13)

As used here, metron refers to the measure, the sphere of influence, or the extent of one's God-given authority.

Every human being has a metron. This is not a term applicable only to Christians. A businessperson's metron includes his business and a teacher's envelops the classroom. Police officers have authority which has been delegated to them by the government. God gives authority to parents over their children. A person has responsibility over all of his possessions, including his car, home, etc. Your metron includes everything over which God wants you to take responsibility.

It is important to note that one person's metron ends where another's begins. In the context of the functioning Body of Christ, a pastor has a metron encompassing his sheep, but that does not extend to another pastor's flock. Furthermore, a shepherd's metron may allow him God-given authority to speak into the lives of the congregation, but that does not mean he should dictate to the sheep what to do with their businesses, families, homes, etc. Each person has a metron, and they are responsible individually before God for that area.

In my own traveling ministry, I have a metron which opens doors for me to influence hundreds of pastors and congregations. When I visit in a certain church, I am ever conscious of the authority which God has given to the local minister. Jesus said that the door to the sheep is the shepherd and the thief comes in some other way (John 10:1). I have seen that if I, as a traveling minister, try to get to the sheep without going through the shepherd, I subsequently may "steal" the sheep away from God's appointed shepherd. In the long run, bad fruit results from such usurping of authority. I can function within my own metron, which covers a broad range, but I must not cross over into those areas of responsibility held by local church authorities.

I also have learned that my metron is for a specific type of ministry. So long as I stay in my calling, God blesses tremendously. However, sometimes individuals in one congregation or another will try to contact me for personal counseling. In other words, they attempt to have me replace their pastor. Every time this happens, I have seen problems develop, so I am careful now, and I take great precautions to avoid being forced into such a role.

Paul wrote that he would not go beyond his metron (II Cor. 10:13). In the context of this passage, he was talking about *not* extending his influence into Christians' lives who were beyond his God-given authority. As I have explained, whenever an individual tries to exercise spiritual influence beyond that which God has given him, evil forces may be activated.

For this reason, a wise leader knows the limits of his metron. Paul recognized those whom God had placed under his charge. Every leader should know which things are "none of his business" and which are his God-given responsibility. This not only eliminates control and manipulative forces, but it also allows the leader to have confidence within his metron. If a leader has an awareness of God-given authority, he will know that the Spirit of God is working in any given situation. This is so important that I like to sit down with leaders and ask them point blank to describe in detail what they perceive to be their spheres of influence.

To know one's metron, a person must be a realist. Sometimes people develop false concepts of their own authority. There are the weirdoes with grandiose ideas who imagine they have world-wide, leader-encompassing metrons, when, in reality, they are unable even to care for themselves or their own families. Again and again, we encounter Christians puffed up with dreams and vain imaginations. Usually, they think they have God-given authority over their pastor or even over many Christian ministers. Such deceptions (in varying degrees) are fairly common, and they must be corrected before a person can live effectively as a part of the Body of Christ.

Also, there are the sincere Christians who have felt the call of God to great ministries, but they have not yet grown into the fullness of their calling. We see that Joseph in the Old Testament had a vision from God entailing tremendous authority; however, Joseph did not achieve that influence until years later. King David was anointed by the prophet Samuel as a young boy, but David did not come into his kingdom until he was a man. So, also, there are Christians who have had visions and directives from God concerning far-reaching ministries. We must understand that such pictures of the future are not to be grasped or claimed immediately. Rather, one must grow and mature into them.

Deceptions concerning authority originate with our spiritual enemy, Satan. It is from his nature that the spirit of self-exaltation comes. It is a spirit of this world, in the same way that the lust of the flesh and the lust of the eyes are loosed in this world (I John 2:16). The boastful pride of life must be resisted with the same determination as other temptations. If thoughts of one's own greatness are not defeated, Satan will establish a stronghold in the person's mind and, eventually, use it to steal, kill, and destroy.

Any person can be swayed in his thoughts as a result of the spirit of pride, and all people are, from time to time. Knowledge can lead to arrogance (I Cor. 8:1); plus, as we learned earlier, inactive authority is an open door for deception. We also see that people who have been raised under rejection, or with inferiority complexes, sometimes overcompensate and have a tendency to fall for the related deceptions. Of course, this should not be confused with how God often takes a person's weaknesses and makes them their greatest areas of strength. I am simply are warning against Satan's deception of self-exaltation.

There are many leaders who, as they begin to be admired by their followers, start to accept the praise and enjoy the glory which belongs to God. As they receive such praise, their own thoughts become distorted. They begin to see themselves not as they really are, but through the eyes of admirers who are exposed only to the image portrayed in front of the masses. Sometimes they begin to attribute the anointing of God, the revelation they have, or the success of their ministry to their own labors, rather than to God, and soon the devil has a stronghold in their lives.

Whoever exalts himself will be humbled (Matt. 23:12). This is a promise from God. Every Christian must be taught to reject the spirit of pride. A realistic view of oneself is essential. Paul wrote:

> ...I say to every man among you not to think more highly of himself than he ought to think; but to think so as to have sound judgment, as God has allotted to each a measure of faith.   (Rom. 12:3)

When a person loses sight of Who gave him the gifts and talents he possesses, he loses sound judgment and drifts into deception.

In relationship to metron, every Christian should know where his God-given authority lies. The reality to one's own metron is simple: Where is it presently? Who, indeed, can you influence? Who listens to your words? Do not fool yourself. For what has God given you the responsibility right now? That is your metron. No more—no less.

Once a person has determined the limits of his own present metron, it is his responsibility to fill it—to measure up to that which has been measured to him. This means that we actually are to use our abilities and talents to establish order within the area of our influence. For the Christian, this implies that we accomplish the will of our Lord Jesus throughout the metron given to us individually. A leader must keep his soul poised over all those he oversees.

In church ministry, people come to a church looking for spiritual leadership. A shepherd must provide it. Paul exhorted the elders at Ephesus:

> *Be on guard for yourselves and for all the flock, among which the Holy Spirit has made you overseers....* (Acts 20:28)

People can sense whether or not their pastor is accepting responsibility to watch over their spiritual welfare. If the pastor greets the people with the heartfelt attitude, "I accept responsibility for you," the people can feel it and will come to rest under his care. If the pastor has not accepted responsibility, then they will feel unwelcomed and uncared for as soon as they walk inside the doors of the church.

These principles are especially important in dealing with strong individuals. Wealthy businesspeople, doctors, lawyers, politicians, and other professionals usually have risen to their positions because they already have authority. Ministers sometimes are intimidated by those who carry authority outside of the Church-world. People of authority are very sensitive to that. A doctor or successful businessperson will have a very difficult time looking for leadership from a pastor who cowers in his presence. James exhorted Christians not to treat wealthy people any differently than those less fortunate (James 2:1-4). I have found that authoritative people long for leadership, just as anyone else. After sensing—and maybe even testing— a leader's strength, they greatly admire him if he truly cares for them. On the other hand, if they go to a minister for guidance, and that minister will not accept responsibility for their spiritual welfare, they feel disillusioned and sometimes betrayed or hurt.

I like to tell pastors "to get bigger." Not only are there successful people in the secular world looking for spiritual leadership, but there also will come into their congregations men and women who have had much religious training and experience. An individual who at one time has pastored a large congregation, then retires or takes secular employment, can be very threatening to a young minister. Every leader must rise above the intimidation and become what he needs to become. Only then will the people stay content among the congregation.

I have observed many distinctions between ministers who are successful at leading large congregations and those who struggle with small ones. One of the differences is that ministers overseeing large congregations have authority, and they use it to direct individuals. The minister who has not matured is afraid to use his authority. He lets misbehavior and various problems slip by unaddressed. He would rather not hurt anyone's feelings. Confrontation is difficult for him. In contrast, the successful minister over a large church *sees his job as directing people.* Correction and rebuke are no big deal. In fact, in the same way that a carpenter sees sawing, nailing, and constructing walls as a part of his job, the effective minister sees directive communication as his day-to-day responsibility. These are completely different attitudes evident in ministers of large and small congregations.

I would like you to see such corrective activity as accepting responsibility for one's metron. Only if you are responsible with what you have been given will God give you more. In the parable of the talents (Matt. 25:14-30), our Lord explained that the man who uses his talents will be put in charge of many things. In another passage, He said:

> *For whosoever has, to him shall more be given; and whoever does not have, even what he has shall be taken away from him.* (Mark 4:25)

"To have," in this context, means to embrace and accept. The person who embraces God-given responsibilities today will be blessed, and his metron will be expanded by God tomorrow. On the other hand, every time a person shrinks back from responsibilities, his sphere of influence diminishes.

God's leaders for tomorrow's world are those who fill their metrons today.

This is how authority works. Some people have an idealistically unreal concept of authority. They want God to appear to them someday and put them in charge of some great ministry. They want to be famous overnight. They pray that God instantaneously will bless their business, financial situation, or overall position in life. They perceive of God as a Santa Claus, passing out gifts indiscriminately.

I would like to compare that mind-set with what I call "a poverty mentality." Many people never are able to get ahead financially because they have certain ways of thinking established in their minds that restrict and blind them. We could point out many such thought patterns which enslave a person to poverty (I discussed them in another book entitled, *Developing a Prosperous Soul),* but let me emphasize just one that is very common. People who never seem to be able to prosper financially very often have their hopes set on some grand provision or opportunity coming their way. Their heart longs to win the million-dollar lottery, receive a large inheritance, invent the gadget everyone wants, find a get-rich-quick scheme, or be discovered by some wealthy individual who believes in their hidden talents. I like to call such a mind-set "the lottery mentality." People who have it never seem to get ahead until they give up and redirect their hearts.

Sometimes Christians have a "lottery mentality" when it comes to successful leadership. They want to be discovered. They want some famous person who is already in a position of authority to recognize their gifts. They even pray for a miracle to happen. I have known ministers who have their hopes set toward receiving a large donation, being asked to preach before a huge audience, getting that key building in the center of their town, or having God work an amazing healing. In error, they think that if they just had that big opportunity, then their ministries would be successful and they would be recognized. People with such thought patterns rarely, if ever, become effective leaders.

Please do not misinterpret what I am saying here. I believe in miracles, God supernaturally elevating a person, large donations being given to various ministries, and unexpected opportunities appearing. However, these boosts into individuals' lives come to those who already are working toward their goals. When a person has a mind-set that he will give his life serving God, whether or not God ever does a miracle or supernatural act, then God acts: "...to him who has shall more be given." Miracles come, provisions appear, opportunities arise in the life of the person whose heart is set toward fulfilling his/her God-given responsibilities.

God also acts on behalf of those who "minister down," rather than those who are reaching for the stars while neglecting their present responsibilities.

For example, in a church there will be some individuals who ambitiously have their eyes set on ministering to the whole church from the pulpit, but they never have been successful at ministering to the few individuals just around them. Others, more wise, will minister to the people just around them, and, in time, they shall be asked to come "to the head of the table." This principle is just as true in the workplace. Every person has a metron and when they take care of their present responsibilities, then God will exalt them. In contrast, the person who has their eyes set on reaching up or outside their metron, will be humbled repeatedly.

Many Christians never have grasped this basic truth. They dream about ministering to kings and presidents. They want to travel the world and own great wealth. They naively think God will anoint them with tremendous power and authority if they just have enough faith. In reality, they will waste their days with a metron that reaches no further than the people they presently are helping.

*If you want to go up, take care of what is below. The more you put under your feet, the higher you will climb. Again, I say, **minister down**.*

Right now there is a metron which already has been given to you. It is under your authority. If and when you establish the order of God throughout your metron, then God will add more to you. Keep your eyes and your energy focused on developing what God already has given to you.

Concerning ministry, work with people who *want* your ministry. Sometimes that is humbling. You may want to reach the famous and influential, but the only people who want to hear from you are the insignificant and unnoticed. But if you faithfully minister to those who presently are hungry for your words and touch, someday the famous and influential also will want your touch.

As a young minister, one of the most helpful statements I heard from an influential man of God was: "Nobody is going to give you a ministry; you have to build it." Of course, there are times that God does elevate a person or enlarge a person's work quickly. But for the most part, that is not how He works in our lives. In fact, He warned Timothy in the Bible not to exalt any person too quickly into leadership "lest he become conceited and fall into the condemnation incurred by the devil" (I Tim. 3:6). The plain truth is that God follows His own advice.

God works in our lives as a vine dresser carefully laboring over His vineyard (John 15:1-11). He helps us to grow. He prunes us when we start growing outwardly too fast. He deepens us in His ways day by day, step by step.

The question may be asked, "How can I become an overnight success?" The answer is to work hard, never quit, and 50 years from today forget all the nights between the beginning and the end. That's reality. Start today, and by the end of your life, you will be able to look back and say that you have done all God put you here to accomplish.

Chapter Eleven
Trusting the Anointing

We have seen how the spirit of a person flows outward and enlightens his thoughts (I Cor. 2:11). I would like you to see this principle in conjunction with the truths I just discussed about a person's metron. When God has given a person responsibility for some area (his metron), He will give him the ability to manage it. The spiritual life within will emanate outward and reveal that which is needed to accomplish the tasks at hand. That is what authority offers to a person.

Parents have responsibility for their children. With that responsibility, there is also a sense of knowing what to do with one's offspring. For example, a mother naturally desires to care for her loved ones. A father is motivated from within to protect and provide for them. Of course, there are people who are emotionally disabled and others who have rejected their natural responsibilities and denied those instinctive behaviors, but we recognize that desires to love and care for one's children are normal.

Similarly, a businessperson has a "knowing" inside which helps to manage his or her own business. If, indeed, God has delegated to a person the responsibility to oversee that business, He will give the person the authority—which implies the ability—to do the necessary work.

Whatever a person's metron, they will have authority to manage it. That is what it means to have been given a metron. The person's eyes and ears are opened, and he becomes sensitive to what is happening within his area of responsibility. In addition, they have the understanding within as to how they can influence, correct, or direct circumstances and people within their metrons. Such knowledge may not be complete, but as an individual steps out to act on what he knows should be done, progressive understanding is given and answers become evident.

The wise person learns to trust the God-given perception and understanding in line with his metron. The successful businessperson is the one who not only works hard, plans, and is faithful, but also is quick to respond when an unexplainable knowing directs him down a specific path. The mother who senses in her heart that her child needs to talk is always wise in taking the first step. The seasoned police officer follows his senses which tell him where to go and what to do. A homeowner who feels unsettled about something pertaining to his home should investigate and discover if there is, indeed, a problem. Pertaining to our subject of leadership, leaders must not be led merely by logic and experience, but also by the "knowing" which rises within their hearts.

These truths are critical when it comes to ministry in the Body of Christ. The anointing of God causes one's metron to encompass some aspect or dimension of the Church. The Holy Spirit then activates and flows out with the Christian's spirit, bringing God's enlightenment and revealing truth.

In line with this principle, John wrote:

> ...*the anointing which you received from Him abides in you, and you have no need for anyone to teach you; but as His anointing teaches you about all things, and is true and is not a lie, and just as it has taught you, you abide in Him.*
>
> (I John 2:27)

We are told that the anointing will teach us. It will show us what needs to be done. It will provide answers when problems arise. It is true. We can trust it.

Please examine this carefully. Only if you know that it is your anointing—or in other words, the working of the Spirit of God within you Who is revealing things to you—will you be confident to act, speak, and step out in authority. If you have questions about yourself, you will be hesitating and feeble in your actions. If, however, you know that it is God who has positioned you over a specific business, organization, project, home, or ministry, then you will be able to exercise the authority, direction, and influence which God wants you to exercise. Therefore, you must see these truths both in the Bible and functioning in your life.

Now, understand your anointing as working within your own natural being. Sometimes Christians have a very limited concept of how God leads people. They imagine that the voice of God must come from heaven in a deep thundering tone. God could speak that way—in fact, He did more than once in the Bible.

However, when we talk about the anointing within a person, we are talking about the Spirit of God rising within a person and revealing things to him. The Spirit inspires thoughts, helps an individual see what he needs to see, directs his attention to important things necessary for work, management, change, etc. The anointing usually quickens a person's natural functions so that he simply can work more effectively and efficiently.

To understand how God works through the anointing, compare it with the evil counterpart of how the devil works in people's lives. The devil tempts people. That is, he puts his thoughts in their minds, and they decide whether or not to receive them, that is, believe them and act upon them. At the time a person is tempted, he usually does not know whether the evil thought was simply his own fleshly desire rising within, or whether, in fact, it was a devil inspiring the thought. In similar fashion, when God inspires thoughts and desires through the anointing upon a Christian's life, he may not know whether it is God, or simply a good thought which he has had. The anointing is within (I John 2:27). It teaches people. It is, therefore, very much a part of one's natural makeup and difficult to separate from oneself.

Every great leader learns to trust that which is within him—the anointing, the knowing, the divine guidance, the Spirit of God, the authority which God has deposited within. Self-confidence is God-confidence in the area of one's anointing. I am not teaching any self-exaltation doctrine here, nor am I opening the door for egotistical domination. I am

simply stating that no leader will be effective unti
believes that God is at work inside of him.

Dwight Moody, the famous evangelist who shook
America and Europe during the late 1800's, said,
"Almost everything I ever did in my life that was a
success was done on the impulse."* The word
"impulse" here is referring neither to emotional nor
erratic behavior, as the term often is used in the
negative sense today. On the contrary, Mr. Moody was
describing a lifestyle of yielding to the divine guidance
within. He learned to trust it. He realized that there
was more guiding his life than just his own intellect.
To this he accredited his success.

Leaders must be confident that there is more at
work in their lives than just their own natural
strengths. *To be successful, confident, bold, and able to
make decisions, they must come to the point of deciding
that they simply will yield to that which is flowing
within.* When they come to the point of realization
that God is leading them, 90% of their doubts and
fears are dispelled. When they learn to yield to the
anointing, then they release the anointing which they
have.

Furthermore, the working of God within a person
changes his heart. Paul wrote:

> *...for it is God who is at work in you, both
> to will and to work for His good pleasure.*
> (Phil. 2:13)

---

* William R. Moody, *The Life of D.L. Moody* (New York: Fleming
H. Revell Co., 1900), p. 46.

Think of God literally at work
now. He is there in you. He really

at God is doing inside you? He is
work changing your desires. He is making you
"want" to please Him. He is stirring you to serve Him.
Ezekiel spoke out God's promise concerning the inner
workings of the Spirit:

> And I will put My Spirit within you and
> cause you to walk in My statutes, and you
> will be careful to observe My ordinances.
> (Ezek. 36:27)

God is inside of Christians by His Spirit, causing,
stirring, and even pushing them to fulfill His will.

Do you see what this means? You cannot live to
your fullest in God unless you grasp this truth.

Many Christians have a negative concept of their
own walks with God. They see their own human
desires directing them down one path, and God's
desires for their lives directing them down an entirely
different path. They think that the way to please God
in this life is to do what they really do not want to do.

That way of thinking is contrary to the Gospel and
the working of God in our lives. God is not dealing
with us in a legalistic fashion, where He is telling us
what to do and then expecting us to conform our own
lives to it. He is inside of us causing us to "want" to do
His will. The heart of the Christian is the heart
through which God reveals His desires. The mind of
Christ manifests through the mind of the Christian.

If you are a Christian, then you must not see your thoughts and heartfelt desires as contrary to God's. They are not in conflict. Of course, you will have some things arise in you that are not entirely according to His nature. But for the most part, the longer you walk with God, the more your own thoughts and desires will be His.

This means that to fulfill God's call upon your life, you ultimately must do that which is in your heart. Let me be very bold and say that when you start doing what you really want to do, then you will be doing what God wants you to do in life.

I believe this truth to such a degree that I consciously let my heart lead me to accomplish God's will. At times I get so involved in my work that I lose sight of where I am going. Instead of stopping everything and forcing myself into some mold which I have in my mind of God's will for my life, I usually ask myself, "Harold, what do you want to do right now?" In order to ask this question, I had to come to the point of believing that God is the One Who is at work in me, causing me to want to please Him. Do I really believe that He is at work in me? If I do, then my heart is the primary channel through which He leads me.

No man or woman ever will be a powerful leader for God until they discover this truth. If they always think of their own desires as contrary to God's, they will live in doubt and unbelief. They will be in conflict with themselves. They never will know, with clarity, God's will for their lives.

Now in saying this, I want to warn my readers again. We are not giving credence to any person satisfying his own evil lusts. Any and every person can have thoughts arise in them that are not of God. However, that possibility for error is no reason to discard your own thoughts and feelings. What it should do is cause you to unite with other Christians who can judge and evaluate you.

Every person needs others to keep them in line. Leaders must have others they can trust—off of whom to bounce ideas and with whom to discuss things. The foolish leader surrounds himself with people who will agree with everything he says (commonly known as "Yes Men"). The wise leader keeps strong men and women nearby who are not afraid to challenge and correct attitudes and ideas. Having such people around does not undermine leadership, but gives greater confidence to the key leader, because he knows others will bring necessary correction. Godly relationships are the best safeguard from deception.

Even though I am giving only one paragraph to mention the need of relationships, please do not think I am minimizing their importance. Many other books have been written on this subject, and I am fully convinced of the importance of Godly relationships. Here, however, my aim is to focus upon the leader, and with that aim, please allow me to proceed.

Look again at your heart and how God wants you to govern your life. The Apostle Paul wrote:

> *...God has allotted to each a measure [metron] of faith...And since we have gifts that differ according to the grace given to us, let each exercise them accordingly....*
> (Rom. 12:3-6)

God does not want you doing things all of your life that you do not like doing. What you are supposed to be doing is what comes by *grace* to you. That is what God is calling you to do. Grace is the power and favor of God working on your behalf. Where that grace is for your life is where you ought to be.

Let me put it in other terms: you cannot be a successful leader unless you are seeing your dreams realized. Of course, there will be trials and challenges. It even may be terribly stressful at times. However, if you are doing God's will, then, overall, it will be enjoyable to you. You will be fulfilled in it. If you are not having any fun, then you are doing the wrong thing.

Chapter Twelve
The Heart of the Leader

If God, indeed, has given authority to a person, then that authority implies the ability to release blessings upon others. The man or woman who understands these truths can be used powerfully to accomplish the will of God in other's lives.

To begin, let me relate a situation I experienced in a church I pastored several years ago. As many other ministers have experienced, I watched many people come and go through the congregation. It seemed that every time a few new people would join, in a short time a few others would leave. I experienced the "revolving-door syndrome," which is very frustrating to pastors.

After a few years of overseeing that congregation, I started noticing a pattern. Before some person would leave my church, I would become unusually conscious of them. I would be burdened for them, or a thought would come to my mind that they were struggling in their lives. Then, sure enough, a week or two later they would leave the church and go somewhere else, or simply drop out of fellowship. At the time, I did not associate this "knowing" in my heart with the anointing in me, but after seeing this again and again, I started to recognize a connection between the people leaving and their first coming into my heart in a troubling way.

One day in frustration, I cried out to God for the answer to this dilemma. After praying for a long period, I was led to the Apostle Paul's words, where he said:

> *For I am confident of this very thing, that He who began a good work in you will perfect it until the day of Christ Jesus. For it is only right for me to feel this way about you all, because I have you in my heart....* (Phil. 1:6-7)

Years earlier I had memorized the first part of this passage, which speaks of being confident of God's ongoing work and protection in another person's life. However, that day I saw a connection between this work of God and how Paul declared that "he had the people in his heart." The reason or the basis upon which Paul was confident was that he was aware those Christians were in his heart.

This made sense to me because I had been observing the workings of this principle in my church for months. At first they would come to my heart's awareness, and then it was as if they would "slip out" of my heart. After I let them go from my heart, they would leave the church. There was a spiritual connection between my heart and the work of God in their lives.

When I realized this, I went to war! The Bible tells us that we fight not against flesh and blood, but against the evils of darkness (Eph. 6:12). Believing this, I called a fellow leader in my church to come together with me to pray for those people who had left our congregation over the previous months. We interceded for each one of them by name. We asked God to begin working powerfully in each of their lives, and we kept praying for each one until we felt that they were "back in our hearts."

The results were nothing short of miraculous. The day we first prayed in that fashion was a Saturday, and the very next day several of the people we had brought back into our hearts were sitting in the midst of the Sunday morning congregation. The second Sunday a few more joined in. No special effort was made to contact or reach any of them. They simply showed up. God did it!

Eureka! I had discovered a principle that had been written clearly in the Bible all along. We are told that the issues of life flow from the heart (Prov. 4:23). We do have the power to bind or loose. Since God had given me authority at that time to shepherd His people, I had His authority, to some degree, to release His blessing upon their lives. The anointing within me was teaching me all I needed to know concerning for whom I should pray and in whom God was presently at work, causing growth and maturity. My confidence in their well-being was dependent upon my holding them in my heart.

At this point, I need to bring in our understanding of metron. As I explained earlier, we each have limits to our God-given authority. Regarding bringing people into our hearts, we must not go beyond our metron. Paul wrote to the Corinthian Christians:

> *But we will not boast beyond our measure
> [metron], but within the measure
> [metron] of the sphere which God has
> apportioned to us as a measure [metron],
> to reach even as far as you. For we are not
> overextending ourselves....*
>
> (I Cor. 10:13-14)

Paul understood the limits of his metron, and he
explained that he would not go beyond it. As I have
been teaching throughout this book, to go beyond
God-given authority is to release evil forces. The extent to which you can exercise God's power ends
where His delegated authority ends. Therefore, it is
wrong for a Christian to extend his influence beyond
what God has ordained for his life.

Regarding pulling people into your heart, it is
wrong to pull in people for whom God has not given
you authority. For a pastor to draw in people who
belong to the church down the street would be to
violate God-given authority. God also will move some
people out of a certain congregation, and in such cases
if a pastor continues to hold them spiritually, he will
be resisting God. What we are saying is that a leader
must be sensitive to the Holy Spirit.

Leaders must take responsibility for those over
whom God, indeed, has made them responsible. Jesus,
in speaking to the Father, said of His disciples:

> *While I was with them, I was keeping
> them in Thy name which Thou hast given
> Me; and I guarded them, and not one of*

them perished but the son of perdition,
that the Scripture might be fulfilled.
(John 17:12)

Jesus "guarded" over those who were given to Him. He kept them. It is in this fashion that the leader of God's people must hold those given to him within his heart in the Name of Jesus.

Seeing these principles, I decided to make myself intensely aware of what was going on in my own heart. As the leader of a congregation, I realized that the authority I had was real. It was not just an imaginary thing. It existed in the spiritual realm. Therefore, it was my responsibility to hold those God had given to me within His blessings. I decided not to let anyone out of my heart. As a result, the "revolving-door syndrome," which I experienced as a young pastor, was diminished. During that first year of diligently applying this truth, my church greatly increased in size, and I was no longer guilty of losing those God had placed in my care.

Of course, as I explain this spiritual principle, we must understand that every person has authority over his own life. Jesus, Himself, lost Judas, who chose to go his own way. In my own church, even though I continued to hold my congregation within my heart, a few did stray in their walks with God. Each person still does have a free will.

As I taught in Chapter Two, there are four distinct lines of authority in the earth: to the individual, to the family, to the Church, and to the government. In the discussion here, I simply am talking about leaders using the authority God has given them for their people. I am not implying that leaders have total or complete authority over those they lead. On the contrary, every person is still responsible to God for his own life. I am talking about only one of those lines of authority and trying to help you see that it is, indeed, real. Therefore, please understand these truths in light of all I have been teaching to this point.

These principles are just as true in family relationships. Parents have God-given authority over their children. A father and mother who hold their children in their hearts are releasing God's blessing upon their children. Blessed is the man whose grandmother has his picture above her hearth where she can be continually reminded to think of him, pray for him, and cherish him. The blessings of God flow through the heart of a person, and where the heart is directed, the blessings flow.

I have seen the reality of this in my own family only too often. I know that my parents pray for my well-being every day and I am grateful for that. As head of my own family, I, too, attempt to keep my soul poised for the welfare of my loved ones. In my ministry I travel extensively, sometimes without my wife and children. My wife and I learned a long time ago that her welfare is dependent to some degree upon my releasing God's blessing, even if I am gone from home. There have been times that I have forgotten my family for a time, especially after traveling and becoming very busy ministering. Sometimes I get so busy that I unconsciously let them slip out of my heart. I have observed that those are the very times that trials seem to come upon my unprotected loved ones. When I finally get to the telephone to call my wife, she will tell me that the car broke down, or the children were especially wild, or she had a disagreement with some friend. My wife is so in tune to this truth that if things start going wrong while I am away, she will call me just to remind me to pray and cover the children and her. It works. It really does.

Parents and all leaders with authority need to realize the intimate relationship between their hearts and those over whom they have been given authority. Let me say it again, "Authority is real."

Satan and all the demons know this. A demon cannot decide on his own initiative when or whom he will destroy. If God has given authority to a human being, then those demons must obtain the permission of that person before they can attack and accomplish their goals to steal, kill, and destroy. A person has authority over his own life, so they decide for themselves whether or not to listen to temptations and submit to the devil. Also, there is authority which comes through ordained leadership, and the devil has to seek the permission of the person in charge before he can do his work.

For example, Jesus explained that at one point Satan demanded permission to sift Peter like wheat (Luke 22:31,32), but Jesus prayed for Peter that his faith would not fail. Notice that Satan was demanding permission from our Lord to sift Peter. Jesus did not give the devil permission, but instead prayed strength into Peter.

Examine the authority which the Apostle Paul

demonstrated when he did allow the devil to destroy a sinful man. A certain man in the Corinthian church was living in immorality, and he would not repent. Even though the Apostle Paul was not in the city of Corinth at that time, he wrote:

> *For I, on my part, though absent in body but present in spirit, have already judged him who has committed this,....I have decided to deliver such a one to Satan for the destruction of his flesh....*(I Cor. 5:3-5)

Notice that Paul judged this man, that is, he turned his heart against him, and thus removed the protection he had as a spiritual father to the Christians involved there. As a consequence, the devil had access to this man's outer vessel, and he was subject to destruction.

Now, I am not advising Christians today to release the devil on other people, as the Apostle Paul did in this case. I simply am helping you to realize how the spiritual principles of authority operate. Paul had authority over the church at Corinth, and he was dealing with a very serious case of sin and rebellion. Had he been present at Corinth, he would have kicked that evil man out of the church (I Cor. 5:2). However, since he was distant, he decided to exercise his authority from right where he was. He did this in the name of Jesus Christ, as God was directing him to do (I Cor. 5:4). The reason he could exercise this authority is because God had given him authority. These were his children in the faith.

People today sometimes release the devil and various trials upon their loved ones without knowing it. Being unaware of how authority works, they sometimes remove the protection they are supposed to provide.

Usually, when the devil comes to seek permission to destroy, his request will be so subtle that the individual with authority will not recognize it as a request for permission to do evil. For example, if the devil comes to work in your own life, he does not speak audibly or announce to you that he is the enemy and wants to destroy you. Rather, he offers you something such as he offered to Adam and Eve. He tempts you. It sounds reasonable or even good. You then make a decision whether or not to receive or believe that which he says.

In similar fashion, the devil's request to destroy those you love comes in the form of a subtle thought. The idea may come to a pastor that Joe, who has been a long-standing member of his congregation, is not doing very well. Or this pastor may have the thought recurring in his mind that Sister Sue is mad at him, and, therefore, he is better off without her. The unaware leader may accept such a thought and, as a result, lose faith for that individual. By accepting and believing such a thought, the leader may allow the person to slip out of his heart and may, therefore, withdraw the spiritual protection and blessing that he/she should secure.

Similar workings are seen in the family situation. Satan does not walk up and ask a mother if he can destroy her daughter. He tries to obtain permission subtly. He does this by offering thoughts which will cause mom to give up hope for her daughter. He will tell the mother over and over again that her daughter is rebellious, and that she is not going to make it in life. When the mother finally has accepted such thoughts, she has—whether or not she realizes it—given the enemy permission to destroy. Of course, that daughter still has authority over her own life, but the mother has been tricked into removing her spiritual blessing and protection.

It is the attitude of faith and confidence that releases God's blessing and authority into others' lives. The wise father and mother must take faith for their children. A leaders must not allow negative or hopeless thoughts of their disciples. If any person arises within his heart in concern, the leader should pray that the person's faith will not fail. The person with authority must hold his people within his heart. Only then can the leader be confident that God is at work within them, finishing the work that He began (Phil. 1:6-7).

Finally, it is important that we make room in our hearts for all people, especially those in the family of God. Paul asked all the Christians at Corinth, "Make room for us in your hearts..." (II Cor. 7:2 NAS). We understand that we can exercise authority only over those whom God has given us, however, we can bless any person simply by directing our love and faith toward them.

Jesus explained that when we hold unforgiveness against one another, we hinder the forgiveness of God in our own lives (Matt. 6:14-25). First John 3:15 tells us that a brother who directs anger toward another brother is a "murderer," that is, he is robbing his spiritual life and releasing forces of destruction. In contrast, when we forgive and direct our love toward one another, we release God's blessings. We protect each other from the enemy's attacks.

We must understand that whatever we bind is bound and whatever we loose is loosed. It is by our holding others in our hearts and always maintaining faith for one another that we release God's blessings. Believing the best releases the best. As I believe for you and you believe for me, we release God to finish the work which He has begun in us.

Chapter Thirteen
Leaders Are Different

Jesus told a parable about how a first man was given one talent, a second two talents, and a third five talents (Matt. 25:14-30). He went on to say that each received the talents according to his own ability. Then after explaining how the first two did not use their talents, while the third did, our Lord taught how every person will be judged according to how he uses that which is given to him.

Several truths can be learned from this parable, but first—clearly shown to us—is that different people are entrusted with different gifts and abilities. Even from birth, we possess certain talents that will enable us to accomplish what God has put us here to do. Some people have talents in one area and others in another. Some people have tremendous natural abilities, while others seem to be less gifted.

The reason I point this out is to emphasize that people are different. That may seem obvious to you, but if I word it differently, this truth may shock you. Let me put it this way: "All men *are not* created equal." Please do not take this in the wrong way. Every human being is created in the image of God, deserving of love, respect, care, provision, opportunity, etc. However, we are *not* created with the same gifts and talents. In that sense, we are not equal.

In our focus upon leadership, we must recognize that leaders have certain gifts that others do not possess. Some leadership skills are developed through training and experience, but if God, indeed, has placed a certain individual upon this earth to fulfill a leadership role, then he or she will possess essential characteristics from birth.

Beyond natural abilities, there is also the call of God. When an individual surrenders his life to Jesus, God breathes new spiritual life into him. God writes His laws and desires upon the heart of the new Christian. What is written upon the heart of one Christian is not the same as God inscribes within another. Of course, each believer has written within a code of holiness and a standard of living to please the Father. However, God's unique plan for that individual's life also is planted within the Christian. What is written upon your heart is what God wants you to accomplish in this world. What is written upon a different Christian's heart is what God desires him to accomplish. As the Father gives birth to each of His children, the desires of God concerning their individual lives are instilled within them.

So, a Christian leader is different, not only by creation and natural abilities, but also because of the God-given calling upon his life. Deep within the heart of the leader there is a desire to lead. It changes the way he looks at life...influencing values, priorities, daily decisions. The heart of the leader is focused in a different direction than the average person.

Let's make a natural comparison. A mother with children is different than a woman who never has had to care for little ones. They both deserve love and respect. Both are human beings. However, a mother is different in the way she thinks, the attachments of her heart, and her very purpose in life. A mother makes decisions all day long based on how they will affect the lives of her children. A sense of responsibility pervades her life and influences every thought. Her sense of motherhood determines what she does, who her friends are, where her time is spent, etc. A mother's heart is directed toward her children. She is very different in character and nature than a woman without children.

The same could be said for the eldest child in a family. Typically, the eldest grows up with a sense of responsibility that younger siblings do not share. Of course, there are exceptions, but very commonly the eldest carries an uncanny awareness for the well-being of the rest of the family. If someone suffers in the family, he or she carries the burden more intensely than the others. The sense of responsibility compels them to become more involved, more helpful, more supportive. The eldest is different than those children growing up without a position of responsibility.

If we can accept the fact that a mother and an older child are unique in character, then we also should be able to understand that a man or woman called to leadership is different. They are distinct in thought-life, heart motivation, sense of responsibility, purpose, direction, drive, gifts, talents, etc. It is that simple. If you are a leader, you are different than the people around you.

This is no small issue. In the Churchworld over recent years, we have tried to break down the walls between clergy and laity. This has been for good reason. During Church history, the ministers, priests, and pastors became so distant from the common people that a wrong was being committed. Churchgoers were becoming both inactive and separated from any intimate relationship with God. Much teaching over the past hundred years has helped to change that and to develop within all Christians an awareness of their own ministries and their roles in fulfilling the purposes of God in the earth.

However, there is a danger evident in over emphasizing these truths. Many leaders have lost any sense of what it truly means to be called of God. In Acts 13:2, we read about the Holy Spirit speaking to the church leaders of Antioch and saying, "Set apart for Me Barnabas and Saul for the work to which I have called them." There is, indeed, "a setting apart." In the attempt to elevate the average congregational member, leaders have, in many ways, lowered their own standards and diminished the respect once held for God's calling to leadership. *In no way do we wish to lower the saints back to a place of uninvolvement or insignificance. Rather, we need to raise both the leader and the follower to a higher standard of ministry.* It is now time to speak to leaders and tell them again about the sanctity of God's precious calling which does, indeed, separate them from the average churchgoer.

I personally know enough leaders, truly called of God for ministry, to say without any shadow of a doubt, that they are different. Every Christian has a heart to please God, but not everyone goes to bed at night wondering how he or she can help people. Nor does every Christian have the perspective of seeing the people of God as sheep without a shepherd. Only a person with a calling to leadership knows what it means to take a shower, drive his car, mow the lawn, go shopping,...while at the same time burdened for the Church. I have cried with enough pastors, evangelists, teachers, and other leaders to know they have a different piece of the heart of God than the person without a call to these ministries.

If you are called to be a leader, you must answer the call. You can kick against the goads and resist God, as Paul did for a time (Acts 26:14), but God still remains there—nudging, urging, creating dissatisfaction within you; constantly making you aware of needs and the greater responsibility laid upon you. You never will be content sitting inactively in a pew. Working 40 to 60 hours a week at a regular job, living just to build a home and raise a family, will never be enough. There is no way to escape it. The gifts and calling of God are irrevocable. To do in this world what God put you here to do is the only thing that will make your life fulfilling, joyful, and blessed.

Mario Murillo, in his book, *Critical Mass*, put it this way:

> ...to do anything below what you were
> created to do will bore you.

It is not enough just to be saved. It is not enough to experience the power and workings of the Holy Spirit.

Of course, these are central issues in the Christian's life, but unless one goes on to become what he is created to become, and do what he has been placed here to do, he never will be fulfilled in this life.

A call to leadership has tremendous implications, not only for this life, but also for the next. The Bible tells us that leaders will be judged more harshly than others (James 3:1). For those who prove faithful, great rewards are reserved. Paul wrote of rewards promised to those who win souls, teach the Word, disciple others, etc. Of course, salvation from hell is given by grace, but beyond that, our eternal destiny is determined by what we do in this life. We sometimes refer to the great blessing reserved for the sweet little grandma who prayed for years, or the faithful church custodian who cleaned the toilets without a complaint. Of course, there are rewards laid up for every Christian who has served our Lord faithfully while on this earth. We do not want to lessen the significance of everyone's service to God, but it is time we face reality concerning judgment. Jesus explained in the parable of the talents that people will be rewarded according to how they use their gifts (Matt. 25:14-30). He who has much, and uses it, will be given much more. Those who are candidates for harsh judgments are also candidates for great rewards. One does not come without the other. Jesus told the apostles that those who walked faithfully with Him would sit on thrones judging the 12 tribes of Israel (Luke 22:30). Make no mistake about this truth. God has His eyes upon the leaders of His people. Those who prove faithful will receive great rewards for eternity.

Let's review. Leaders are born with certain gifts and talents which distinguish them from others. Written upon their hearts they have a plan from God which guides them in specific directions. The ongoing work of the Spirit never will let them be content to live as ordinary men and women. They look at people and life differently. They see needs and feel compelled to do something. For eternity, leaders who are faithful to their calling will receive from God rewards far surpassing those who are faithful with lesser gifts.

Some Christians, those content to sit passively in the pews, may object to what I am teaching here. The average person who never has experienced the call of God may not like to think of any brothers or sisters in the Lord as in a different class. But I boldly declare that the separation is real. Set 100 Christians in a room, and I will tell you which ones are called to be leaders simply by inquiring about what they have been thinking. Being a leader means something. It is not just a title. If you are a leader, you are different.

This does not give any basis for self-exaltation. Pride is evil. Please do not take these words in such a wrong manner. You still are subject to temptations, as any man or woman. Your salvation still is based upon the same grace of our Lord Jesus Christ. It is only by His choice that you will stand.

When we talk about a distinction between leaders and those they lead, we are not implying any exalted position or deserved privileges. The distinction to which we are pointing primarily is related to responsibility. Leaders carry a sense of responsibility for others. They also are responsible to God to use the gifts they have been given. Their individual callings demand that they "measure up" and give their lives for others. This is the distinction I want you to recognize.

Chapter Fourteen
The Making of a Leader

Jesus took fishermen, rebels, a taxcollector, and ordinary men and made them into leaders. Certainly our Lord recognized the potential of those men. Yet, He had His work cut out for Him in taking those disassociated independents and creating a team that would turn the world upside down.

First and foremost, they were united around Him. They believed in Him to such a depth that they were willing to leave their homes and businesses. They recognized the Messiah—the hope for all people.

But Jesus did more than captivate their hearts. He revealed His heart and He imparted His heart to them.

To see this, consider what He did before laying hands on the 12 and sending them out to preach (Matt. 10:1-7). Just before their first commissioning, we see our Lord on top of a hill with His disciples gathered around Him:

> *And seeing the multitude, He felt compassion for them, because they were distressed and downcast like sheep without a shepherd.* (Matt. 9:36)

Picture this: The disciples had been following Jesus

for several months at this point. He had been moving from one community to another, healing the sick and preaching to the multitudes. One day as Jesus looked over the people, He was moved with compassion. The Greek language from which these words were translated imply that Jesus groaned from His innermost being. With His disciples gathered around Him, He was consumed with love for the people. In that moment they saw His heart.

Then Jesus turned to the 12 and said:

> *"The harvest is plentiful, but the workers are few. Therefore beseech the Lord of the harvest to send out workers into His harvest."* (Matt. 9:37b-38)

I envision Jesus kneeling down upon that hill and crying out to the Father. He then asked the disciples to join Him in prayer. Overwhelmed with the needs of the masses, they saw the harvest. At some point, the disciples must have seen the people the way Jesus saw the people. Not only did they see His heart for people, but they saw the people as "sheep without a shepherd."

Immediately after that experience, Jesus called the disciples to Him, laid His hands on them, and gave them authority. He then commissioned them to go out to preach to the multitudes (Matt. 10:1-8). Indeed, they went forth from there with such authority that they not only preached the good news but they cast out demons and healed the sick.

The disciples did not receive the commission nor

authority of our Lord until they saw and embraced the heart of our Lord.

There is the key: when you receive the heart of God for a specific people, then you will receive the anointing of God to minister to those people.

Let me give you some examples. When I first was put in charge of a small congregation, everyone called me "pastor." To be honest, I was not anointed as a pastor. I had the official credentials, but for the first few months I simply was filling a position. I taught the people and carried out the expected responsibilities, but I did not have special love for those people. I just as easily could have pastored a different congregation in some other town. But then one evening, after several months serving in that position, a woman from the congregation telephoned me to tell me that her husband was leaving her. Other than listen and express my concern, I did not know what to do. After I hung up the phone, I began to cry, not only for her, but for every marriage in the church and for every person. That evening something changed in my heart. The Holy Spirit did a work in me. I accepted responsibility before God for those people. They became my flock and I became their shepherd. Though I had been called "pastor" for quite some time, I became their pastor that day. I can look back today and recognize how the people began to treat me differently from that day forward. They recognized my heart for them.

On another occasion I saw the heart of a Christian leader whom I greatly respect. After he taught several thousand people in a huge auditorium, I had the privilege of going to eat a meal with him. We were in a fancy restaurant, where everything was done proper and dignified. Shortly after our meals were served, this man of God who sat across the table from me began to cry. His head dropped into his hands and right there in the most elegant surroundings, he began to sob. I heard the words he muttered through his tears: "Oh, God, no one cares! No one is helping the people!" It was at that moment I knew why God was using him to lead tens of thousands of people to Himself.

I travel to many nations now and I have similar experiences regularly. Upon my first visit to a people, I observe them, touch their lives, and see their struggles. At some point, I become consumed in their needs and desires. Each time, God allows me to sense His love for the people. I know now that unless He reveals His heart in me, I never will be empowered to help them as He desires me to do.

This same principle works in all leaders. In fact, I have worked with some who have lost their passion. They confide in me that they no longer desire to minister. They do not sense the leading of God anymore. They want to quit.

On more than one occasion I have sat with a disillusioned minister and talked to him about the people—their needs, their pain, their dreams. After refocusing the heart of a leader, desires return to help those people. A heart of compassion positions a leader's heart in the right place where inspired thoughts, vision, and drive begin to flow.

I apply this principle every time I get ready to

speak to a group of people. I do it when I write. I know that if I think about the needs of the listeners, and I pray to God to help me see the people the way He sees them, then my own thoughts will become illuminated. God will breathe His ideas into me. I will know what to say or write. The anointing will lead me. God's answers and blessings will flow through me.

Years ago when I was young, I used to dream about living in Bible days. I imagined how it would be to walk on the dusty trails with Jesus. Most of all, I wish I could have been there when He laid hands on the first 12 disciples. How wonderful it would have been to hear Him call the names "Peter, John,..." then to hear my name called. If I could have been there to hear His words and receive His authority, then I, too, could go out to change the world.

In reality, it is not necessary for me to go into the past. Our Lord is in the present. He is here. He promised to go with us even to the ends of the world. He gives us His authority (Matt. 28:18-20). He is with me. His hands are on me. His Spirit is in me. He has commissioned me.

And He is with you, right now.

111

Books That Will Change Your Life
by Harold R. Eberle

THE COMPLETE WINESKIN (Fourth edition)

The Body of Christ is in a reformation. God is pouring out the Holy Spirit and our wineskins must be changed to handle the new wine. Will the Church come together in unity? Where do small group meetings fit? How does the anointing of God work and what is your role? What is the 5-fold ministry? How are apostles, prophets, evangelists, pastors and teachers going to rise up and work together? This book puts into words what you have been sensing in your spirit. (Eberle's best seller, translated into many languages, distributed worldwide.)

TWO BECOME ONE (Second edition)
Releasing God's Power for Romance, Sexual Freedom and Blessings in Marriage

Kindle afresh the "buzz of love." Find out how to make God's law of binding forces work for you instead of against you. The keys to a thrilling, passionate, and fulfilling marriage can be yours if you want them. This book is of great benefit to pastors, counselors, young singles, divorcees and especially married people. Couples are encouraged to read it together.

THE LIVING SWORD

"The truth shall set you free." So then why does Christian fight Christian over doctrinal issues that seem so clear to each side? Can both be right, or wrong? Learn how Jesus used the Scriptures in His day and then apply those principles to controversial issues currently facing us such as women in the ministry, divorce and remarriage, prosperity, God's plan for our lives,.... What we need is the leading of the Holy Spirit on these subjects. This book will bring the Scriptures alive and set you free.

GOD'S LEADERS FOR TOMORROW'S WORLD

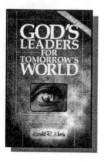

(Revised/expanded edition) You sense a call to leadership in your life, but questions persist: "Does God want me to rise up? Is this pride? Do I truly know where to lead? How can I influence people?" Through a new understanding of leadership dynamics, learn how to develop godly charisma. Confusion will melt into order when you see the God-ordained lines of authority. Fear of leadership will change to confidence as you learn to handle power struggles. Move into your "metron," that is, your God-given authority. You can be all God created you to be!

PRECIOUS IN HIS SIGHT A Fresh Look at the Nature of Man
During the Fourth Century Augustine taught about the nature of man using as his key Scripture a verse in the book of Romans which had been mistranslated. Since that time the Church has embraced a false concept of man which has negatively influenced every area of Christianity. It is time for Christians to come out of darkness! This book, considered by many to be Harold Eberle's greatest work, has implications upon our understanding of sin, salvation, Who God is, evangelism, the world around us and how we can live the daily, victorious lifestyle.

YOU SHALL RECEIVE POWER

Moving Beyond Pentecostal & Charismatic Theology
God's Spirit will fill you in measures beyond what you are experiencing presently. This is not just about Pentecostal or Charismatic blessings. There is something greater. It is for all Christians, and it will build a bridge between those Christians who speak in tongues and those who do not. It is time for the whole Church to take a fresh look at the work of the Holy Spirit in our individual lives. This book will help you. It will challenge you, broaden your perspective, set you rejoicing, fill you with hope, and leave you longing for more of God.

DEAR PASTORS AND TRAVELING MINISTERS,

Here is a manual to help pastors and traveling ministers relate and minister together effectively. Topics are addressed such as ethical concerns, finances, authority, scheduling,…. In addition to dealing with real-life situations, an appendix is included with very practical worksheets to offer traveling ministers and local pastors a means to communicate with each other. Pastors and traveling ministers can make their lives and work much easier by using this simple, yet enlightening, manual.

DEVELOPING A PROSPEROUS SOUL
VOL I: HOW TO OVERCOME A POVERTY MIND-SET
VOL II: HOW TO MOVE INTO GOD'S
FINANCIAL BLESSINGS

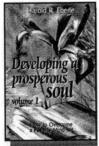

There are fundamental changes you can make in the way you think which will help release God's blessings. This is a balanced look at the promises of God with practical steps you can take to move into financial freedom. It is time for Christians to recapture the financial arena.

SPIRITUAL REALITIES
Here they are—Harold R. Eberle's series explaining
how the spiritual world and natural world relate.

VOL I: THE SPIRITUAL WORLD AND HOW WE ACCESS IT
Here is a scriptural foundation for understanding the spiritual
world. Learn how to access that world,
touch God, and experience His blessings. Be
aware of the dangers and false manifestations.
Release God's power into your life and the
world around us.

VOL II: THE BREATH OF GOD IN US
A study on the nature and origin of the
human spirit, soul, and body. Knowing
God's activities within our being. Understanding the spiritual
energies which God releases in us to think, be physically healthy,
and be sucessful.

VOL. III: ESCAPING DUALISM
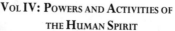
Understand how God created you to live as a whole human being:
redeeming the soul, knowing God's will, sanctifying "soul power"
and finding freedom as a child of God. This
book will set you free!

VOL IV: POWERS AND ACTIVITIES OF THE HUMAN SPIRIT
God created you in His image, with His
breath. Discover what this means in relation
to your creative powers, spoken words, dreams, and experiences
in space/time. Here is a Biblical explanation of spiritual
phenomena.

VOL V: SPIRITUAL DYNAMICS BETWEEN PEOPLE
What is going on spiritually between you and the people around
you? Now you can understand spiritual bonds, authority streams,
group consciousness, family dynamics, the
power of free will and covenants.

VOL VI: THE NATURE OF CREATION
The spiritual and natural worlds overlap.
This has profound implications for our un-
derstanding of Creation, the origin of life and death, the nature of
time, laws governing our universe, how our thoughts influence the
natural world, and much more.

WORLDCAST MINISTRIES

A significant portion of the profit from book sales goes to the support of Christian missions, Bible colleges, charitable work, and orphanages in developing countries around the world. This work is done through the oversight of Worldcast Ministries, which is an organization overseen by Harold R. Eberle and a staff of volunteer and paid workers. Worldcast Ministries is a ministry based on the belief that God is raising the Church up to a position of unity, maturity, and glory. We believe that the greatest revival the world has ever seen will take place between now and the Second Coming of our Lord Jesus Christ.

The Bible Colleges which Worldcast Ministries founds and oversees are growing around the world. These are interdenominational Christian schools graduating several hundred ministers each year. These ministers plant and establish churches primarily in poorer and unreached areas of the world.

If you are looking for something meaningful in which to be involved, we welcome your financial support and we encourage you to join us in helping fulfill the Great Commission to go and make disciples of all nations.

WORLDCAST MINISTRIES
P.O. BOX 10653
YAKIMA, WA 98909-1653
E-mail: office@worldcastpublishing.com
Web Site: www.worldcastpublishing.com